CRYPTOCURRENCY AND NFT TRADING

Step-by-Step

*The Best Investing Guide For Monetizing
With Non-Fungible Tokens.
Learn How To Use Cryptocurrencies
To Create, Buy And Sell Nfts
Discover The Future!*

D1571091

information contained in this book. This warning applies to any loss, damage or injury caused by the application of the contents of this book, directly or indirectly, through wrongdoing, negligence, personal injury, criminal intent or under any other circumstance.

You agree to accept all risks arising from using the information presented in this book.

You agree that by continuing to read this book, when appropriate and/or necessary, you will consult a professional before using the remedies, techniques, or information suggested in this book.

TABLE OF CONTENTS

ANDREW Mc.COIN

My name is Andrew Mc.Coin, I am 38 years old and I am an American trader, investor and author of finance books. I was born and lived in Philadelphia, and at the age of 20 I met the person who, without ever knowing it, would change my life forever.

At that time I worked in a famous fast food chain, I was on duty very often in the morning or afternoon until late in the evening. It was not a satisfying job, indeed it was very stressful and I did nothing but dream of going out a few nights with my friends or going on vacation. But for me life was that: getting up, going to work, resting a bit, hanging up with the evening shift and going to sleep... and the next day, repeat. Without prospects.

One evening a friend of mine, Scott, whom I had not seen for some time, came to dinner in the place where I worked, accompanied by other friends of his that I did not know. I remember that meeting and that conversation as if it were time! It was very late, and just then I was finishing my shift, so Scott and his friends invited me to sit down with them for a while. As I talked about how tired I was, Scott also complained that he had to get up early the next day for a date. Until Scott asked one of his friends, "And you Win, what do you have to do tomorrow?" At that moment I noticed Vince. He was the most quiet and smiling, seemed satisfied and serene, was well dressed and definitely relaxed. Vince replied, "Nothing, I think tomorrow I'll go to the beach." Scott said, "But tomorrow is Wednesday, don't you work?" He replied, "Yes, but I can choose when to work." At that point I asked, "What work do you do?" Vince replied, "The trader." Another friend of Scott's asked Vince, "But do you make good money?" Vince replied, "Yes, if you're a good trader, but the best part is that the time you invest in the job is free from the economic gain you make, that is, you can earn even when you're not working directly at that time."

I knew broadly the profession of the trader, and I did not think it was a profession within my reach, so there for there I did not give weight to that information, and I continued to think only about my life and how boring, stressful and repetitive it was ... Today, going back, I think I could have asked him a lot of questions, but at that moment unfortunately I did not. A few days later, however, while I was always working tired and stressed, Vince's answer began to come back to my mind: "I think tomorrow I will go to the sea." And this phrase kept spinning in my head and I began to think: "How nice it would be to be able to choose every day for your life! How nice it would be to be able - as he said - to free the time you invest in work from the economic gain you get." I wondered, "But will it really be possible to make money even when you're not working?" At that point I wanted to ask Vince a lot of questions, but I never had the opportunity to meet him again. What I didn't know yet was that Vince had already changed my life without even knowing it.

About three months later, walking around a bookstore, a book came into my hands entitled: "Living by Trading", and I thought: "But will it really be possible to live on trading?" I bought that book and read it overnight after work and after that many others, until one day I decided to try on a famous platform that gives the possibility to simulate trading operations with virtual money. To my amazement I discovered that I was good, but above all that I improved by continuing to try. Was I a trader? I never knew if I hadn't tried to get serious! The problem was only one: I had no budget, so I had to get it! For a year I worked putting money aside, in some periods I also did two jobs, tiring, boring and stressful, but I was very motivated, now I saw a new perspective in my life! While I was putting money aside, I kept reading, learning and training on my virtual platform, until I found myself a good nest egg to start with.

It was an endless year, but I still thank myself for doing it. Today I can answer those questions on my own: "But will it really be possible to live on trading?" and "Is it really possible to free the time you invest in work from the economic gain you get?". This is my answer: "Today I have been a trader for 15 years and, yes, every now and then, I open my app to place my offer even while I am on the beach."

My books are the result of 15 years of my work, they contain everything I have learned from my successes, but above all from my mistakes. Within them I concentrated what I wanted to know when I started studying this subject and investing to change my life. I hope that others can gain time, and therefore money, through my experiences. I am not jealous of what I have learned and my strategies, there is room for everyone in the world of Trading, and if you want I wait for you inside!

INTRODUCTION

Great artists concentrate solely on their creations or masterpieces. Musicians spend days or months searching for the perfect lyrics and harmony, architects concentrate on the smallest details on their building plans, and painters search for the perfect place for their final stroke. But once they have completed their masterpieces, successful artists must also figure out a way to monetize them while also safeguarding their provenance and potential future value.

This is where the intermediary comes into play. Content creators of all kinds— from musicians, writers, podcasters, performers, writers, directors, and composers, are often forced to use an intermediary if they want the world to know about their works. Whether it is the music label, the art gallery, or the concert promoter, these intermediaries all assure artists the ability to monetize their work in exchange for a healthy cut of the profits—and in some cases, ownership of the artist's work.

Although not all intermediaries are terrible, some have made headlines in recent years for the highly questionable deals they have made with their clients. Taylor Swift has spoken out about the unjustifiable contract she signed as a teenager as well as how her music was sold multiple times without her consent or knowledge. Musicians such as Prince and Michael Jackson were also known for feuding with their record labels.

In recent years, technology platforms such as Spotify have offered some rays of hope for disintermediation. However, as the platforms evolved, artists discovered that their economics had been reduced rather than enhanced. It is no surprise, then, that the creative community has long sought a way to reclaim control and ownership of their valuable creative assets or properties.

This is where the NFT, a tool that allows creators to completely avoid the intermediary altogether, comes in. Understanding how to use NFT technology can put creators back in control. NFTs appear to be shrouded in cryptocurrency jargon, scaring off anyone without a computer science degree, but they are quite simple. They enable artists to embed a snippet of code into their works, allowing them to share them without worrying about piracy and with the assurance that they will be paid by their supporters and fans in perpetuity. This gives them back power and control of their intellectual property while increasing transparency and tracking and distributing royalties and sales payments to the creator.

One of the most valuable aspects of NFTs is the way they enable a community to form and support something in which they believe. It is clear that not only are NFTs here to stay, but they also have the potential to radically change the content and creative industries. The idea of investing in this market is no longer an imagination, but rather a fundamental strategy for anyone who wishes to make a meaningful contribution to the creative economy.

INVESTING

IN

CRYPTOCURRENCIES

CHAPTER 1: DIFFERENCE BETWEEN TRADITIONAL AND DIGITAL CURRENCIES

Cash, or physical money, is a fantastic thing. You can transfer (or spend or give away) as much of what you own as you want, whenever you want, without any third party authorizing or censoring the transaction or charging a fee. Cash does not reveal sensitive personal information that could be stolen or misused. Unlike digital transactions such as credit card purchases and bank transfers, which are a pain point for merchants, when you receive cash in your hand, you know that the payment can't be 'undone' (or charged back, in industry parlance) at a later date. In most cases, once you have money, it is yours, it is under your control, and you can transfer it to someone else right away. A financial commitment is immediately fulfilled when physical money is shared, and no one has to wait for anything else.

Traditional currencies, which are also known as Fiat currencies, are distinguished because they are not linked to any single country, nation, or institution (in most cases). There are no Bitcoins from the United States, no Litecoins from Japan, and nothing similar. They are decentralized. On the other hand, traditional physical cash has a significant flaw: it does not work at a distance. You can't send physical money to someone on the other side of the room, let alone across the globe, unless you have it with you. This is where cryptocurrency comes in handy.

In contrast to real money, digital money relies on bookkeepers who their customers trust to keep accurate accounts of the balances they hold. To put it another way, you can't directly own and control digital money (well, until Bitcoin came along, but more on that later). To get your hands on digital money, you'll need to open an account with someone else—a bank, PayPal, or an e-wallet. Someone else is a third party you trust to keep track of how much money you have with them—or, more precisely, how much they must pay you on-demand or transfer to someone else at your request. Your account with a third party is a record of your trust agreement: it shows how much money you have with them and how much money they owe you.

Without the third party, you'd have to keep bilateral debt records with everyone, including those you don't trust or who don't trust you, which is impossible. If you purchased something online, for example, you could send the seller an email stating, "I owe you $50, therefore let's both record this debt." On the other hand, the merchant is unlikely to accept this; first, since they have no reason to trust you, and second, because your email is useless to the business—they can't use it to pay their employees or suppliers.

Instead, you advise your bank to pay the merchant, which it accomplishes by reducing the amount your bank owes you and raising the amount the merchant's bank owes them. This extinguishes your debt to the merchant and replaces it with an obligation to their bank in the merchant's eyes. The merchant is pleased because they trust their bank (well, more than you), and they can put the money in their bank account to good use.

Unlike cash, which settles by transferring actual tokens, digital money determines by growing and lowering balances in trusted intermediaries' accounts. This is probably self-evident, though you may not have considered it that way. We'll return to this topic later, as bitcoins are digital money with some characteristics similar to physical cash.

The distinction between online card payments, in which you type the numbers, and physical card payments, in which you tap or swipe the physical card, is significant. An online credit card payment is referred to as a "card not present transaction," but swiping your card at the cashier's till in a store is referred to as a "card-present transaction." Because online (card not present) transactions have a greater likelihood of fraud, you should supply extra information, such as your address and the three digits on the back of the card, to make fraud more difficult. To counterbalance the cost of fraud prevention and fraud losses, merchants charge additional fees for these types of payments.

Unlike many kinds of digital money required by law to demand personal identification, cash is an anonymous bearer asset that does not record or hold identity information. Regulations require that a bank, wallet, or other trusted third party identify you before you may open an account with them. This is why you must frequently provide information about yourself, backed up by independent evidence. Typically, this entails a photo ID that matches your name and face, as well as a utility bill or other "formal" registered correspondence (such as from a government department) that verifies your residence. Identity information is acquired in various ways, not simply when opening accounts. It is also collected and utilized for validation purposes when making electronic payments. When paying online with a debit card or credit card, you must provide your name and address as the first line of defense against fraud.

Bitcoin was created as "deflationary money," which means that its value will, in principle, rise with time. It is not like fiat currencies, which are subject to inflation and whose value will depreciate over time. After all, a dollar in 1917 was equivalent to $20.17 today. As a result, the US Dollar is 20 times less valuable than 100 years ago. To put it another way, if you keep $1 for 100 years, you'll be able to buy fewer and fewer things in exchange for it, whereas with Bitcoin, the opposite will happen.

Another example from the actual world. On May 22, 2010, Laszlo Hanyecz made the first real-world bitcoin transaction. He paid 10,000 BTC for two pizzas in Jacksonville, Florida. 10,000BTC is now worth more than $40 million.

Bitcoin was created in this fashion so that no single person (or government) could raise the supply of money, decreasing the value of existing capital.

We must also remember that the fiat currencies we are familiar with were not always the dominant players in the money market. Gold and other valuable metals have long been regarded as the most desired currencies for everyday use. Coins (and later paper bills) did not become the preferred payment method until governments were able to standardize and verify the metallic content.

CHAPTER 2:
WHAT IS A BITCOIN?

Bitcoin is the first cryptocurrency or crypto currency as well as being the most popular. Its price continues to rise from year to year, making bitcoin a digital asset that is sought after by many people.

Bitcoin is a decentralized digital currency that was created in January 2009. The invention of bitcoin is Satoshi Nakamoto.

Bitcoin is known as a type of cryptocurrency because it uses cryptography to keep it safe. There are no physical bitcoins, only balances stored in a public ledger that can be accessed by everyone transparently (even though every record is encrypted).

In other words, bitcoin is a set of ideas and technologies that serve as the foundation for a digital money ecosystem. Bitcoins are digital money units used to store and transport value among bitcoin network participants. Users of the bitcoin protocol connect primarily over the internet; though alternative networks can also be used. The bitcoin protocol stack, which is open-source software, can be executed on various devices, including laptops and cellphones, making the technology widely accessible.

Users can use bitcoin to do almost anything that can be done with traditional currencies, such as buying and selling items, sending money to people or organizations, and providing credit. Bitcoin can be purchased, sold, and swapped for other currencies at specialized currency exchanges. Bitcoin is, in some ways, the ideal form of internet money because it is fast, safe, and borderless.

Bitcoin, unlike traditional money, is purely digital. There are no actual coins, nor are there any digital coins. Transactions that transfer value from sender to recipient imply the use of cash. Bitcoin users have keys that they can use to prove ownership of bitcoin on the bitcoin network. They can use these keys to sign transactions that unlock the value and be spent by transferring it to a new owner. Keys are frequently maintained on each user's computer or a smartphone in a digital wallet. The only requirement for spending bitcoin is accessing the key that may sign a transaction, putting complete control in the hands of any user.

Bitcoin is a peer-to-peer, distributed system. As a result, there is no "centralized" server or control point. Bitcoins are constructed through a process known as "mine," in which participants compete to solve a mathematical problem while processing bitcoin transactions. Any bitcoin network participant (i.e., anyone with a device running the full bitcoin protocol stack) can function as a miner, verifying and recording transactions with their computer's computing power. On average, every 10 minutes, a bitcoin miner can validate the previous 10 minutes' transactions and is paid with brand new bitcoin. Bitcoin mining, in essence, decentralizes a central bank's currency issuance and clearing activities and eliminates the need for any central bank.

Despite not being a legal tender in much of the world, Bitcoin is very popular and has fueled the launch of hundreds of other cryptocurrencies, collectively referred to as altcoins. Bitcoin is commonly abbreviated as BTC when it is traded.

CHAPTER 3:
THE BITCOIN PROTOCOL

The bitcoin protocol has built-in algorithms that control the network's mining function. The difficulty of the processing works those miners must complete dynamically changed so that someone succeeds on average every 10 minutes, regardless of how many miners (or how much processing) are competing at any given time.

The protocol also cuts the number of new bitcoins issued every four years in half and caps the overall number of bitcoins created at slightly under 21 million coins. As a result, the number of bitcoins in circulation is expected to hit 21 million by 2140. Bitcoin is a deflationary currency in the long run because of its decreasing rate of issue.

Furthermore, bitcoin cannot be inflated by "creating" more money than is intended to be issued.

Bitcoin is the name of the protocol, a peer-to-peer network, and a distributed computing breakthrough behind the scenes. Bitcoin money is merely the first implementation of this technology. Bitcoin is the result of decades of encryption and distributed systems research, and it combines four fundamental ideas into a unique and powerful combination. Bitcoin is made up of:

- A decentralized peer-to-peer network (the bitcoin protocol)
- A public ledger of transactions (the blockchain)
- A set of rules for independently validating transactions and issuing currency (consensus rules)

- A system for achieving worldwide, decentralized consensus on a legitimate blockchain (Proof-of-Work algorithm)

CHAPTER 4: IDENTIFICATION OF THE MAIN CRYPTOCURRENCIES: ALTCOIN

It's straightforward to define what an altcoin is. It's any coin that isn't bitcoin in terms of technicality. Bitcoin is as traditional as this field can get, having been the first to strike the scene and gain a mainstream following. Altcoins refers to the rest of the coins that make up the cryptosphere. Yes, Ethereum and XRP are included. They acquired their name because they offer services, functionalities, and usability characteristics that bitcoin either doesn't have or doesn't want to supply. They also provide crypto enthusiasts with options other than bitcoin in terms of investing.

Within a portfolio, altcoins offer two advantages: protection against bitcoin and the potential for greater interest in the token.

Since the market is new, no one knows what the future holds for any coin in this arena, including bitcoin. While it is currently the most prominent currency, there is no certainty that another coin will emerge to take its place as the crypto's bellwether. If such a coin grew, it would emerge from the altcoin world (unless it was one of bitcoin's splits). While you shouldn't invest in altcoins that you believe will entirely dethrone bitcoin, it's a good idea to have some exposure to a couple of them in case one of them begins to rise as a result of its rising market power, independent of bitcoin.

Corporations are only now beginning to grasp the full potential of blockchain technology. As a result, they're turning to these startup coins to see if they can meet their digital currency needs while maintaining safety, security, and legality. When new blockchains emerge, they will be tested, and the most trustworthy ones will gain popularity with a community beyond the initial investors. These altcoins' prices may climb as a result of this. You can typically get a more significant part of the coins at a lower price because they're significantly cheaper than bitcoin. They also give hope that businesses will latch on to certain coins that bring value to their business via the token's blockchain.

You buy altcoins in the hopes that they will appreciate it. However, there's no guarantee that they will, which is why you shouldn't put your entire crypto portfolio in altcoins. Many coins have done little to demonstrate that the company will become a viable business or that transaction volume will rise at a substantial enough rate to support an investment thesis and justify a greater valuation. They have yet to be proven. Like most unverified investments, your cryptocurrency investment is more likely to fail than thrive.

While it is a great idea to diversify your crypto portfolio with altcoins, keep in mind that they're not the same as any other investment. Cryptocurrencies have a high amount of volatility as a whole. Bitcoin, in itself, experiences substantial ups and downs in a matter of days (or even hours). Unless no one invests in them at all, cryptocurrencies, particularly smaller altcoins, have an even higher level of volatility. If you buy in, it's something you'll have to accept. While some will use this uncertainty to sell as soon as a spike occurs, you shouldn't have to bother too much about the daily ups and downs of these coins if you keep that volatility in mind about your entire crypto portfolio—and your crypto portfolio's place in your overall investment holdings. If you keep track of them daily, you can find yourself sipping champagne one day and taking nausea medicine the next.

Less mainstream altcoins, like the more prominent altcoins covered in previous chapters, will follow bitcoin's path. However, because many of these coins have a smaller value per coin, this results in higher highs and lower lows as investors rush into the names to profit from a bitcoin rise. Speculation is driving these moves rather than something concrete in the coins themselves.

Take Stellar's lumen, for example. It crested immediately after bitcoin's apex, rising from $0.20 per coin in late December 2017 to $0.75 per coin in early January, a 275 percent increase in less than two weeks. It had dropped to $0.20 by the end of March. If transaction volume increases, bitcoin prices may stabilize. However, because these coins are newer and have fewer users, fewer transactions exist. That's why, when prices soar, speculation is at the helm. When bitcoin does well, deduction occurs.

Many altcoins will go months, if not years, without seeing any activity. The coin has a low level of curiosity and chatter. Perhaps they're brand-new coins. Maybe they've been left behind. It's critical to comprehend why some coins are still in the basement. Simply because something is cheap or inexpensive does not imply it is a good deal. The low price maybe since no one will ever use the currency in their right mind. Don't confuse low cost with low quality.

CHAPTER 5:
HOW TO OPEN A WALLET AND MANAGE A WALLET AND AN EXCHANGE

Buying and trading cryptocurrencies required a doctorate in computer science, coding, or hacking before introducing the cryptocurrency exchange. Now that exchanges and digital wallets exist to protect your transaction, it's far more fluid and simple process. However, there will be a few crucial times throughout your transaction trip when you have to make decisions. Your experience, security, and returns will all be affected by which option you take. When you purchase a stock or mutual fund on an exchange, you don't have to do much afterward except maybe print out the transaction record for your accountant. The stock or mutual fund share will not vanish as soon as you walk away from the computer, satisfied with your choice.

When buying a cryptocurrency, however, this is not the case. You must keep some items in check, or the coins will fall into a digital void.

Considering fees are often a percentage of the total amount you intend to buy; how much you will determine how much you pay in fees. Most exchanges will cut the fee percent of the total they need to process the payment if you spend a considerable amount. If you buy a modest amount, you'll almost certainly be charged the highest rate.

Expect to wait a couple of days before you may buy or sell your coins, based on how much you wish to invest. Part of this period is due to the currency itself; purchasing coins like Ripple's XRP is faster because there is no miner to confirm the transaction. As a result, processing times are reduced. On the other hand, Bitcoin would typically operate slower because the community must approve it. While you can lock in the coin's price at the moment of purchase, you won't be able to sell it for a few days. You won't be able to sell the coin if its value suddenly triples three hours after you bought it. It will take a few days to a week for the cash to arrive in your digital wallet. Who knows what will happen by then? Your bitcoin profits may be lost.

The length of time you'll have to wait is also determined by how much you're buying. You could have a significant chunk in a couple of days if you buy a significant portion (or minutes, depending on the exchange). Then it's only a question of whether there's currently enough supply to justify the purchase. Because supply is determined by how many coins are up for sale, there is no guarantee that your investment will have enough supply on the market when you initially process the payment.

When you join an exchange in the United States, you'll have to pick how you'll buy the coins. Because many US exchanges, including the most prominent, Coinbase, do not allow credit card purchases, you have three choices:

- **Add a bank account to your account.**
- **Instead of a credit card, use a debit card.**
- **Arrange for a wire transfer to take place.**

A bank account can be used as the funding source for medium to big purchases. For example, Coinbase allows you to deposit up to $10,000 every week using a bank account. Even if they never get close to that top-level limit, this is a highly safe and cost-effective way for most people to fund their crypto investments.

Debit cards are designed for smaller transactions. Some exchanges cap the amount you can deposit via debit cards at $1,000 each week. However, while using a debit card, be cautious because there are fewer consumer safeguards if the debit card numbers are obtained by malware or a hacker.

Wire transfers are convenient for large, one-time purchases. Without additional authentication, Coinbase has a $100,000 maximum. This amount can be increased, but you must persuade the exchange to pay the amount you wish to send.

Coinbase, the popular cryptocurrency exchange, started to store and spend bitcoins and other cryptocurrencies. It wasn't an exchange but rather a wallet. Coinbase transitioned to exchange as the idea of bitcoin investing expanded, and buyers and sellers held on to their coins more like an appreciating asset than a currency. However, don't confuse it with a wallet, and don't confuse any exchange with a wallet. An exchange is a marketplace where you can purchase and sell coins with other investors. A wallet is used to spend currencies, secure investments, and keep tokens safe from specific threats.

Remembering the private key that identifies your currencies once you've moved your cryptos to a wallet is critical. This string of numbers, letters, or even random words will reveal the location of your coins. It's nearly impossible to get your coins back without the key.

Personal preference has a role in selecting the transaction. There are certain features and user interfaces that you might want in one exchange but not in another. Another consideration while choosing an exchange is security. Because exchange laws are continuously being tightened, you'll want to be sure any platform you utilize has passed the most recent regulatory evaluations. The last factor to contemplate when choosing an exchange is whether you can receive the best pricing for your cryptos. When considering selling your coins, it's good keeping an eye on different exchanges because prices might vary depending on which one you use.

What you want from an exchange is the assurance that if you regularly use it to buy and trade cryptos, you won't lose all of your money if it gets hacked. Due to the lack of regulation around crypto exchanges, there is still no guarantee that an exchange will reimburse you if it experiences a security breach.

Mt. Gox declared bankruptcy after being hacked in 2014. It's still in bankruptcy court, with many investors getting nothing in return for their losses. Coincheck, a Japanese exchange, has repaid a portion of the $530 million in losses it experienced in 2018 due to a similar attack. Whether or not an exchange will compensate for the losses will be determined by the exchange and the amount stolen by the hackers. It's a danger no matter which exchange you use, which is why it's a good idea to store your coins in a variety of places, from several wallets to different exchanges, so that all of your crypto eggs aren't in one basket.

Staying within an exchange located in your nation is pretty straightforward advice for people reading this in the United States. You can quickly discover an American-based exchange that meets your aesthetic criteria while also assuaging some of your security concerns because there are so many to select from. Someone who lives in Japan, South Korea, or Hong Kong is in the same boat. Because these areas have an immense interest in the crypto game, they have local exchanges that have completed the due diligence required at this stage of the crypto lifecycle and will adapt to changing rules.

However, being local makes sense because you'll have an easier time collecting if something goes wrong. If you trade in Japan and you currently reside in the United States, it will be more difficult. You may have to deal with language hurdles if a hack occurs. To collect, you'll also need to get considerably more familiar with the Japanese government and legal system.

While numerous exchanges have come and gone, the following names remain well-known in the United States and elsewhere:

- Coinbase (United States)
- Coincheck (Japan)
- Bitstamp (Luxembourg)
- CEX.IO (London)
- Coinplug (South Korea)
- Korbit (South Korea)
- Kraken (United States)

When you purchase coins on an exchange, you have two options for using them. You have the option of keeping the coins on the exchange or moving them to a digital wallet, giving you complete authority over your investment. Because, as you'll learn throughout this book, exchanges have become regular targets for hackers, keeping them on the exchange isn't necessarily the safest strategy. By doing so, you are putting your bitcoins in the hands of an exchange with only rudimentary regulatory control.

If you're investing a large amount of money, it's highly recommended that you put the coins into a wallet. As the size of your investment rises, it becomes more critical since you could become a target, and a loss would have a more significant impact on your bottom line.

You can store or spend your money in these wallets, as many of them were created to allow you to use the currencies for their intended purpose: purchasing goods.

If you trade frequently, you might want to avoid using the wallets. It's not the best plan (because of fees), but it's something to think about if you're trading with a time frame of hours and don't want to transfer significant funds to and from wallets constantly.

CHAPTER 6:
CHOOSING A WALLET

One of the most actively developing apps in the bitcoin ecosystem is bitcoin wallets. There is fierce competition, and while a new wallet is almost certainly in the works, some wallets from the previous year are no longer operating. Many wallets are tailored to specific platforms or uses, and some are better suited to beginners, while others are packed with advanced functionality. Choosing a wallet is a very subjective process influenced by the user's preferences and experience. As a result, recommending a specific wallet brand or project is impractical.

When it comes to transferring your purchases from an exchange to a wallet, you have a variety of methods to select from. Digital wallets or mobile wallets are available for those using cryptocurrency frequently, allowing you to transfer payments for products or services as you go about your day. Others, who regard this as solely a long-term investment, can discover wallets that will remain utterly offline until you're ready to spend, known as "cold storage."

Here's a summary of some of the wallet alternatives available to give you an idea of what's out there:

- Desktop wallets
- Hardware wallets
- Mobile wallets
- Paper wallets
- Web wallets

Many people utilize desktop wallets because of their capabilities, autonomy, and control. Running on common-use operating systems like Windows and Mac OS, on the other hand, has some security drawbacks because these platforms are frequently vulnerable and improperly configured.

Hardware wallets are special-purpose devices that run a secure self-contained bitcoin wallet. They can be used with a desktop web browser or a mobile device using near-field communication (NFC). These wallets are exceptionally safe and suited for keeping enormous amounts of bitcoin because they handle all bitcoin-related processes on specialized hardware.

The most frequent form of a bitcoin wallet is a mobile wallet. These wallets are frequently a good alternative for new users because they run on Apple iOS and Android smartphone operating systems. Many are designed for ease of use, but fully featured mobile wallets are available for power users.

The keys that govern bitcoin can also be printed and stored for a long time. Even if various materials (wood, metal, etc.) can be utilized, these are known as paper wallets. Paper wallets are a low-tech but highly secure way to save bitcoin for a long time. Cold storage is a term used to describe offline storage.

Web wallets are accessible via a web browser and keep the user's wallet on a third-party server. This is similar to webmail in that it uses a third-party server exclusively. Some of these services use client-side code that runs in the user's browser, allowing them to preserve control of their bitcoin keys. On the other hand, most provide a compromise by seizing ownership of users' bitcoin keys in exchange for convenience. Large sums of bitcoin should not be stored on third-party systems.

Another approach to classify bitcoin wallets is by how autonomous they are and how they interact with the bitcoin network:

- Full-node client
- Lightweight client
- Third-party API client

A full client, sometimes known as a "full node," is a program that keeps track of all bitcoin transactions (every transaction by every user, ever), manages users' wallets, and initiates transactions directly bitcoin network. A complete node is responsible for all components of the protocol and can validate the entire blockchain and any transaction independently. A full-node client consumes many computer resources (for example, more than 125 GB of disk space and 2 GB of RAM), but it provides complete autonomy and transaction verification independently.

A lightweight client, also known as a simple-payment-verification (SPV) client, connects to bitcoin full nodes for access to transaction information, but saves the user wallet locally and originates, validates, and transmits transactions independently. Without a mediator, lightweight clients communicate directly with the bitcoin network without the need.

Rather than directly connecting to the bitcoin network, a third-party API client connects with bitcoin through a third-party system of application programming interfaces (APIs). The wallet can be kept on the user's computer or third-party servers, but all transactions must go via them.

When these classifications are combined, many bitcoin wallets fit into three categories: full desktop client, mobile lightweight wallet, and third-party web wallet. Because many wallets run on many platforms and interact with the network in various ways, the distinctions between different categories are sometimes blurred.

While this primarily covers the most frequent and safe variations, it's crucial to realize that there's almost certainly a strategy for you no matter how you spend or keep your currency.

The term "brain wallet" refers to a different sort of wallet. In this version, you create a key known only to you as the private key, indicating where the bitcoin is. Then, when it's time to spend, you'll use the phrase you've created to gain access to the coins. It isn't hack-proof since humans are imperfect at coming up with complicated enough sentences to avoid a hacker's tactics. You can also forget your coins if you forget the word.

When you acquire a cryptocurrency, you'll receive a public key used on the blockchain to verify that the coin is legitimate. You'll also need a private key to access the exact coin when you wish to sell or spend it. The private key is kept in the wallet for you. If you lose this key, you will no longer access the coin. They virtually vanish because, without the code, the wallet won't be able to locate the currency you're referring to, and you won't be able to show you hold it.

Aside from the brain wallet, there are two other options for storing the currencies. You have the option of linking the coins via an online mechanism, known as "hot" storage, or offline storage, known as "cold" storage. How frequently you spend or sell your coins will determine which form of storage you choose.

Hot Storage

A simple way to know whether or not your cryptos are at risk from hackers is to remember that they're vulnerable to theft if they're online. It doesn't imply it will happen, but placing your investment in a digital wallet raises the odds because not only will the coins be stored online. But you'll also have to submit your personal information to a third party—the digital wallet. You could lose your coins if the wallet company itself is compromised.

So, what's the point of using them? You spend a lot of money. Moving coins from cold storage to online, then back to cold storage is inconvenient. It will take a few minutes in certain circumstances, mainly if you use the hardware technique, which involves putting them in a device comparable to an external hard drive. People that use coins frequently will likely consider storing them in a digital or mobile wallet, at least for a portion of their portfolio, to make it easier to retrieve them

If you have a large crypto holding, keep only the coins you intend to buy and spend in hot storage. Investing a more considerable amount of your capital in cold storage will help protect it.

Cold Storage

When you keep your coins in cold storage, you're storing them in an account that isn't accessible to hackers. It is the most secure method to store your coins, and it's what you should do with the majority of them.

You can accomplish this using a variety of approaches. First, you can keep them in hardware that resembles a USB drive, which you can upload the key to and then unplug from your computer. This saves the data on the device, keeping it safe from prying eyes (unless someone were to rob you and take the drive). A desktop wallet is another alternative. Some wealthy investors keep a computer on standby at all times, storing their bitcoins and cryptos on the computer's desktop tool. When they need to sell any of their coins, the computer only turns on for a few seconds to complete the transaction.

Another option is to use digital barcodes, often known as QR codes, as a key, which you can print out on paper. This papyrus piece, known as a paper wallet, will store both your public and private keys. It's one of the safest ways to keep viruses off your computer, but if you misplace the paper or the QR code becomes wrinkled beyond recognition, your bitcoins are lost forever

Just because you're in cold storage doesn't mean you're immune to viruses and hackers forever. You'll need to reconnect your coins to the internet in terms of spending or selling them. During these times, your coins are once again vulnerable. However, it does limit the amount of time your investment is exposed.

CHAPTER 7:
ETHEREUM AND ITS
BLOCKCHAIN

When Ethereum is referred to as "the world computer," what does it mean? Let's start with a computer science-focused explanation, then compare Ethereum to Bitcoin and other decentralized information exchange platforms (also known as "blockchains").

Ethereum is a deterministic but virtually unlimited state machine in computer science, comprising an internationally accessible singleton state and a virtual machine that implements modifications to it.

Ethereum is an open source, worldwide, decentralized computer platform that runs innovative contract programs in a more practical sense. It makes use of a blockchain to synchronize and preserve state changes in the system, as well as a cryptocurrency called ether to track and limit execution resource costs.

Ethereum created ether to handle blockchain transactions and raise funds for initial coin offerings (ICOs). Experts and analysts will use the terms ether and Ethereum interchangeably when discussing the cryptocurrency; Ethereum, the firm, has become synonymous with ether the cryptocurrency. However, owning ether does not imply that you own the corporation that operates intelligent contract technology. You're connected because increasing Ethereum use will increase ether transaction rates.

Developers may use the Ethereum platform to create powerful decentralized applications with built-in economic functionalities. It lowers or eliminates censorship and mitigates certain counterparty risks while ensuring high availability, auditability, transparency, and impartiality.

The first blockchain, Bitcoin's blockchain, keeps track of the state of bitcoin units and who owns them. Bitcoin can be thought of as a distributed consensus state machine, with transactions causing a global state shift and changing coin ownership. After multiple blocks have been mined, the state transitions are controlled by consensus rules, allowing all players to (eventually) converge on the system's shared (consensus) state.

Ethereum is a distributed state machine in its own right. Ethereum, on the other hand, tracks the state transitions of a general-purpose data store, i.e., a store that may hold any data expressible as a key-value tuple, rather than only currency ownership. An arbitrary value can be stored in a key-value data storage.

Ethereum is a distributed state machine (DSM) as well. Ethereum, on the other hand, tracks the state transitions of a general-purpose data store, i.e., a store that may hold any data expressible as a key-value tuple, rather than only the state of currency ownership. A key-value data store stores arbitrary values that are individually referenced by a key, such as the value "Mastering Ethereum" referenced by the key "Book Title." This is similar to the data storage model of Random-Access Memory (RAM) utilized by most general-purpose computers in several ways. Ethereum has a memory that holds both code and data, and it tracks how this memory changes over time using the Ethereum blockchain. Ethereum, like a general-purpose stored-program computer, can load and run code in its state machine. Ethereum can load code into its state machine and run it, recording the resulting state changes in its blockchain, just like a general-purpose stored-program computer. Consensus rules manage Ethereum state changes, and the state is distributed globally, which sets it apart from most general-purpose computers. "What if we could monitor any arbitrary state and program the state machine to build a global computer that runs on consensus?" Ethereum answers.

CHAPTER 8: DECENTRALIZED APPS AND SMART CONTRACTS

Decentralized Apps and Smart Contracts

A DApp (Decentralized Application) is a partially or wholly decentralized application.

Consider all of the possible decentralized components of an application:

- Backend software (application logic)
- Frontend software
- Data storage
- Message communications
- Name resolution

Each of them could be centralized or decentralized in some way. A frontend, for example, can be created as a web application that runs on a centralized server or as a mobile application that runs on your device. Private servers and proprietary databases can be used for the backend and storage, or you can use a smart contract and peer-to-peer storage.

There are numerous benefits to developing a DApp that a traditional centralized design cannot offer:

Resiliency

A DApp backend will be fully distributed and managed on a blockchain platform because an intelligent contract governs the business logic. A DApp, unlike a centralized server-based application, will have no downtime and will be available as long as the platform is up and running.

Transparency

A DApp's on-chain nature allows everyone to scrutinize the code and be more confident in its functionality. Any interaction with the DApp will be recorded in the blockchain for the rest of the time.

Censorship resistance

A user will always communicate with a DApp without interference from any centralized authority as long as they have access to an Ethereum node (and can run one if necessary). Once a smart contract is put on the network, no service provider or even the smart contract owner may change the code.

Backend (Smart Contract)

Smart contracts are used in DApps to store the application's business logic (program code) and related state. A smart contract can be considered a server-side (or "backend") component of a conventional program. Of course, this is an oversimplification. One of the most distinguished differences is that any computation performed in a smart contract is costly and limited to a bare minimum. As a result, it's critical to determine which parts of the program require a secure, decentralized execution platform.

Smart contracts on Ethereum allow you to create architectures. A network of intelligent contracts calls and sends data between each other, reading and writing their state variables as they go, with only the block gas limit limiting their complexity. Many other developers could reuse your business logic after deploying your smart contract.

The inability to update the code of a smart contract once it has been deployed is a crucial consideration in innovative contract architecture design. It can be removed if designed with an accessible "SELFDESTRUCT" opcode, but it can't be altered in any way other than that.

The size of the app is the second most crucial factor to consider when designing an innovative contract architecture. The deployment and use of a massive monolithic smart contract could cost a lot of gas. As a result, certain apps may choose off-chain computing and a third-party data source. However, keep in mind that relying on external data (e.g., from a centralized server) for the DApp's basic business logic means your users will have to trust these other resources.

CHAPTER 9:
TRADING AND INVESTING IN CRYPTOCURRENCIES

Anyone with bitcoins can sell them to you. You can also sell bitcoins to anyone interested. Fortunately, there are several sites where you may locate a group of people eager to trade at reasonable prices—exchanges.

Bitcoin or cryptocurrency exchanges, like stock exchanges, are facilities (typically websites) that attract traders. You do not, however, purchase bitcoins via the exchange. A cryptocurrency exchange is a site that enables people to buy and sell between themselves, similar to a stock exchange where you buy shares from another exchange user rather than the exchange itself. The exchange is simply a meeting place for buyers and sellers, and people go there because they know they'll get a good deal. The exchange is simply a venue for bringing buyers and sellers together, and consumers gather there because they know they'll receive the best deals.

The exchange is an order matching engine in the financial services industry. It brings together buyers and sellers. It also serves as the clearing counterparty for all transactions. Customers can remain anonymous since all matching deals appear to be against the exchange rather than between them directly. Finally, the exchange is the custodian of cash and assets. Customers' fiat money is held in their bank account, while cryptocurrencies are held in its wallet.

What Exactly are Cryptocurrency Exchanges and How Do They Work?

Exchanges are located in many countries and support a variety of fiat currencies and cryptocurrencies. They all work similarly and follow the same four steps:

1. Create an account
2. Deposit
3. Trade
4. Withdraw

Create an account. You must first open an account to utilize an exchange, just as you would with a bank. Because they handle enormous sums of money, exchanges are becoming increasingly scrutinized by regulators. The largest cryptocurrency exchanges match billions of dollars in daily buys and sell. Most legal exchanges follow a similar account opening method to banks, in which new customers submit personal information and proof of identity, such as a passport or utility bill. In a progressive risk-based approach, the documentation required may become more onerous in proportion to the value of cash or cryptocurrency you wish to exchange. These practices are taken seriously by exchanges since they are now a huge business.

Your account is established once the trade is completed. After that, you can log in and proceed to deposit.

Deposit. You must first fund your account before attempting to purchase or sell anything on an exchange. This is comparable to opening a standard trading account before being permitted to purchase traditional financial assets.

Bank accounts and bitcoin wallets are available on exchanges. To fund your account, go to 'Deposit' and follow the on-screen instructions. If you're funding your account with fiat currency (probably to buy bitcoin), the exchange will show you a bank account to which you may send fiat money. If you're loading your account with cryptocurrency (probably to sell for fiat currency or trade for another cryptocurrency), the exchange will show you a cryptocurrency address where you can send your funds.

The balance will be reflected in your 'account balance' on the exchange's website once the exchange has identified the transfer to their bank account or cryptocurrency address, and you will be ready to trade.

Trade. You can now trade up to the amount you've put down. For example, if you deposit $10,000, you can buy up to $10,000 worth of cryptocurrencies. You can sell up to 3 BTC for money or another cryptocurrency available at that exchange if you have deposited 3 BTC.

Prices are expressed in pairings that look like this: BTC/USD or BTCUSD with a figure like 8,000 in them. 'One unit of BTC costs 8,000 USD,' to put it another way. Not all currencies can be traded for each other; the exchange determines which pairs are available. For example, you might see BTCUSD and BTCEUR as trading pairs, which means you can trade BTC for USD and BTC for EUR, but you won't be able to trade USD for EUR if you don't see EURUSD. To convert USD to EUR in that situation, you'd have to sell USD for BTC and then buy EUR with the BTC.

You'll see a screen with bids and offers from other users. These are the prices at which they are willing to trade and the amount of money they are willing to exchange for that price. You can choose to match their prices, resulting in a matched trade, or you can place your own orders, which will sit in the order book until someone matches your price (if they ever do).

Since this is a financial market, the higher the amount you wish to buy or sell, the lower the prices will be. This is not like a supermarket, where buying in quantity gets you a discount. Some people find this perplexing at first, but it is simple to understand. When you buy something on an exchange, the exchange will automatically pair you up with the individual selling it for the lowest price. You must discover the next best deal, which will be slightly higher, once you've purchased everything they have to offer. When you sell something, the exchange matches you with the person who is willing to pay the most for it. You'll have to go to the next highest price, which will be slightly lower, once you've sold as much to them as they want to buy.

Withdraw. Finally, you'll want to cash out in either fiat or cryptocurrency. To accomplish this, you must tell the exchange where you want it to go. If you're withdrawing fiat, you'll need to provide the exchange with your bank account information so they can make the transfer. If you want to withdraw cryptocurrency, you must provide the exchange with your cryptocurrency address so that they can complete the transaction. Because most exchanges feature 'hot wallets,' as stated earlier, which facilitate the process of sending tiny amounts of bitcoin back to users, cryptocurrency withdrawals are usually processed faster than fiat withdrawals.

CHAPTER 10:
BITCOIN LENDING

Unlike most other cryptos, the investing community has, for the most part, shown a desire to at least test the waters in the bitcoin pond. Investors can trade futures contracts, wagering on whether bitcoin will rise or decline, on a futures market that has been formed. Bitcoin has been invested in by electronically traded funds (ETFs) in order to ride the momentum waves and provide a return buffer. The investment bank Goldman Sachs has launched a bitcoin trading division. Moreover, the SEC has been approached by a number of firms seeking permission to create the first crypto index funds aimed at individual investors, which would be significantly weighted toward bitcoin. It's the one crypto that's sparked all of this interest, as it boosts adoption rates while also providing security, putting a bottom under your investment.

While all cryptocurrencies have an interest in how they are perceived and promoted, none has a more substantial image or fan base than bitcoin. T-shirts, souvenirs, bumper stickers, and even actual gold coins have all been created around it. It stands for something far broader than itself: decentralized currency, independence from a central government, isolation, technological success, and wealth, all bundled up in a single term. It has evolved into a status symbol as well as a cryptocurrency. Because the imagery helps sell bitcoin's utility, it helps protect it as the dominant coin within the crypto realm.

What you seek in the cryptocurrencies you prefer, and what you anticipate to see from excellent performing names will determine how you develop fundamentals for your crypto investments. As a result, the basic fundamentals that you notice will vary depending on your personal tastes. When assessing bitcoin, you should take that in mind as well. However, because it is a decentralized currency, there are several fundamentals that you must at least be aware of. Whatever the case may be, you will need to understand how and why bitcoin's currency adoption has improved. If it hasn't grown, you need to figure out why. Aside from that, there are a few more fundamentals that most investors will be aware of.

The amount of potential new coins that could join the market decreases as bitcoins are mined. The current hypothesis is that this will eventually lead to a tightening of the coin's supply (remember, supply is limited), resulting in price hikes for bitcoin, assuming demand continues at current levels (or hopefully increases). It's unclear whether this idea will hold true, as there is a slew of other cryptocurrencies on the market that could affect supply, lowering the impact. However, bitcoin investors won't know if this is beneficial until the market reaches a position where this dynamic can be realized.

Expect a price increase as supply tightens and investors prepare for this possible outcome. At Bitcoin.info, you can keep track of the number of bitcoins in circulation, which is updated daily as new coins are discovered.

More transactions are required for significant price increases in bitcoin. However, you can't have those transactions without giving mainstream users other ways to buy and spend coins. If the number of companies taking bitcoins and the manner in which users may spend them increases significantly, the coin will be better protected against a loss of value, resulting in price increases.

Setting up Google Alerts, which will notify you when there is a change in bitcoin usage, is an excellent idea. To start receiving these alerts as they become published content, go to Google.com/Alerts and type in search terms like "now accepting bitcoin" or "will accept bitcoin." (You can also choose to receive them only once a day, so your inbox isn't overrun with notifications.)

Keep an eye on new legislation

The most severe underlying danger to bitcoin's price is what will happen if official's crackdown on its use. It's something that some countries have done, prohibiting the use of money for local purchases entirely. Russia, for example, has taken a harsh line against cryptocurrency, restricting individuals' access. China, likewise, has made it practically hard for anyone to exchange money. Meanwhile, countries such as Japan, South Korea, and the United States are all working on legislation that may either stifle bitcoin use or make it a safer entity, boosting adoption rates.

If bitcoin use continues to rise, no investor can predict how future policy will look. However, you should be aware of the current laws that govern bitcoin fluctuations. BlockchainLawGuide.com, which provides a helpful breakdown of the current legislation and rules for your crypto investment, can help you comprehend what laws have been placed in place.

CHAPTER 11:
CRYPTOCURRENCY MINING

Defining cryptocurrency may generate responses ranging from "the money of the future" to "the largest bubble since the DOTCOM bubble," depending on who you ask. Senator Thomas Carper of the United States put it best in layman's words.

"Virtual currencies, maybe most notably Bitcoin, have piqued the interest of some, instilled dread in others, and perplexed the rest of us."

Cryptocurrencies are just currencies that do not have a centralized lender, such as a country's central bank, for a more exact definition. They're made with computer encryption techniques that limit the number of monetary units (or coins) made and then verify any financial transfers made after they're made.

Since it is theoretically comparable to mining gold or other precious metals, this creative approach is referred to as "mining." To mine bitcoin, one must solve a growing number of increasingly tricky algorithms or puzzles. Solving these algorithms necessitates a significant amount of computing power. To put it another way, mining them requires money, so we can't just produce value out of thin air. As a result, rather than any central government or bank, the principles of mathematics safeguard these currencies and their value.

As the number of people using bitcoin grows, so does the number of people who use it in real life. Physical goods, gift cards, sports tickets, and even hotel reservations can all be purchased using cryptocurrency. It is now accepted as a form of payment in a number of bars and restaurants. A number of non-governmental organizations (NGOs) now accept Bitcoin and other cryptocurrencies as well. There are also more nefarious uses, such as Silk Road and AlphaBay, which are underground web markets that deal in illegal commodities.

These currencies have numerous advantages over the currencies we are familiar with and use today. That's what makes them so appealing to long-term investors as well as short-term traders. Of course, cryptocurrencies, like any other investment, have some disadvantages.

The Mining Process

One difference between digital coins and, for example, the US dollar is that when a new cryptocurrency emerges, there is usually a defined limit on the number of coins available. For example, bitcoin has 21 million coins that may be mined within its code, and mining these coins requires a lot of energy and computational power. Around 80% of those coins have been mined in total. There will never be another bitcoin after the twenty-first millionth coin is drawn out of the code.

This adds an investment element, which is common in commodities like gold and oil. Because such natural resources are finite, the supply that reaches the market is constrained. When it comes to the dollar, there is no such thing as a ceiling. The Federal Reserve can alter the quantity of money in the economy by increasing or decreasing the amount of money in circulation. This is done in the hopes of controlling inflation or combating deflation—many crypto aficionados like the lack of a governmental monopoly on the token supply.

What is Mining?

The majority of blockchains used to produce and host cryptocurrencies are peer-to-peer networks, which means they work with the help of nodes or a group of computers that all host the blockchain's code. This allows the code to exist in the digital world. However, the peer-to-peer network has a broader scope because these computers also assist in transaction approval. They are compensated with user fees for approving transactions. They also get the new coins that are unlocked as a result of the transactions they approve.

The word "blockchain" comes from the fact that the files within the code resemble a succession of blocks. In actuality, a block is a term used in the blockchain that refers to a file that contains a set of transactions. Consider it one ledger page (and remember, since the blockchain is a digital ledger, it has an infinite number of pages). The miners authorize transactions, and if enough has been approved to fill a block, it is confirmed on the code chain. The miner is rewarded with a Proof of Labor challenge, which is the blockchain's technique of demonstrating that the miner's work produced enough energy (in this case, computational power) to warrant payment. This Proof of Work is essentially an algorithmic puzzle that must be solved by the miner's computers. The miner receives a new coin after it is solved.

The Complexity in Bitcoin Mining

Miners are the first to possess new currencies; thus, they want to sell them so that the supply of bitcoins can meet the demand from regular users. You don't have to mine coins to own them, but it's a helpful notion to understand to help you distinguish between the benefits and drawbacks of each coin's mining methods.

While the most easily obtained bitcoins have already been mined, finding new ones requires a significant effort. In many situations, warehouses loaded with computers running scripts to disentangle another coin are open 24 hours a day, seven days a week. These small businesses, which are generally run by a single person, can deplete a town's energy supply. Due to the sheer impact on local energy resources, some small towns and localities have outright prohibited coin mining. Mining operations in Iceland were predicted to consume more energy in 2018 than the total amount of electricity required to keep all of the country's homes illuminated.

The supply has tightened as mining becomes more profitable—if the price of a currency rises. The coin's value should theoretically rise as a result of this.

Mining operations get more profitable when the price of cryptos rises, making it more advantageous to use more power and search out new coins. Cryptocurrency expert Alex de Vries estimated in 2018 that miners would find it profitable to utilize 64 terawatts of electricity per year based on bitcoin's price. That's more than Switzerland's total population.

The term "mining" is a little deceptive. It draws our attention to the reward for mining, which is the new bitcoin created in each block, by invoking the extraction of valuable metals. Although this reward encourages mining, the primary goal of mining is not to earn money or to create new coins. If you merely think of mining as the process of creating coins, you're mistaking the process's methods (incentives) for the process's objective. Mining is the process that allows the decentralized clearinghouse to validate and settle transactions. Mining is the invention that distinguishes bitcoin, a decentralized security process that serves as the foundation for peer-to-peer digital cash.

Mining protects the bitcoin system and allows for network-wide consensus to evolve without the need for a central authority. Miners are rewarded with newly minted coins and transaction fees as part of an incentive model that matches their actions with the network's security while also implementing the monetary supply.

The goal of mining isn't to generate additional bitcoins. That is how the incentive system works. The technique by which bitcoin's security is decentralized is known as mining.

New transactions are validated by miners and recorded on the global ledger. Every 10 minutes on average, a new block containing transactions that occurred since the previous block is "mined," adding those transactions to the blockchain. Confirmed transactions are those that become part of a block and are uploaded to the blockchain, allowing new bitcoin owners to spend the bitcoin they acquired in those transactions.

In exchange for the security offered by mining, miners receive two types of rewards: new coins minted with each new block and transaction fees from all transactions contained in the block. Miners compete to solve a challenging mathematical problem using a cryptographic hash method to receive this prize. The Proof-of-Work solution is included in the new block and serves as proof that the miner put out substantial computational work. The bitcoin security model is built on a competition to solve the Proof-of-Work algorithm to earn a reward and record transactions on the blockchain.

Mining is the name given to the process since the reward (new currency generation) is supposed to mimic diminishing returns, similar to precious metal mining. Mining creates Bitcoin's money supply, similar to how a central bank creates new money by printing banknotes. Every four years, the maximum quantity of freshly minted bitcoin a miner can add to a block drop (or precisely every 210,000 blocks). In January 2009, it was 50 bitcoins every block. Then in November 2012, it was reduced to 25 bitcoins for each block. In July 2016, it was halved once more, to 12.5 bitcoin. According to this calculation, bitcoin mining rewards fall exponentially until the year 2140, when all 20.99999998 million bitcoins would have been distributed. There will be no more bitcoins issued after 2140.

Transaction fees are also paid to bitcoin miners. A transaction fee may be included in every transaction in the form of a bitcoin surplus between the transaction's inputs and outputs. The winning bitcoin miner gets to "keep the change" on the winning block's transactions. Today, fees account for less than 0.5 percent of a bitcoin miner's earnings, with the great majority coming from newly produced bitcoin. However, as the reward declines and the number of transactions per block grows, fees will account for an enormous amount of bitcoin mining profits. Transaction fees, which will eventually become the critical motivation for miners, will progressively outweigh the mining return. After 2140, the quantity of new bitcoins in each block is zero, and bitcoin mining is exclusively rewarded by transaction fees.

CHAPTER 12:
ICOS (INITIAL COIN OFFERING)

An ICO, or initial coin offering, is a new type of crowdfunding that many blockchain firms are using these days. Patrons can donate in Bitcoin or other cryptocurrencies in exchange for new tokens of the company instead of US Dollars in exchange for shares of the company.

In addition to generating profits for investors, ICOs provide a mechanism for firms to fund their blockchain projects. The offerings usually take a few weeks, and the firm issuing the new tokens will have a target amount they want to raise. In the last 18 months, ICOs have exploded in popularity, and 2017 is on course to be the first year in which blockchain firms raise more money from ICOs than from traditional venture capitalists. In terms of investing, ICOs are a chance for savvy investors to get in on the ground floor of a hot new enterprise.

The disadvantage is that, with so many new ICOs appearing, some of them are significantly less legitimate than others. If you're considering investing in an ICO, make your decision based on the project's core value, not on the company's sales copy's fancy marketing buzzwords. Just because a product or service is built on a blockchain platform does not automatically imply that there is a real-world demand for it. Another aspect to consider is the project's development staff and their track record of producing successful blockchain applications.

More ICOs will fail than succeed, just like any other traditional startup effort, and acquiring funds is only one aspect of a successful project. Bancor, an ICO based on the premise of developing a market-making (producing an automatic buy and sell price) product that provided liquidity for digital assets, is one example of an ICO with issues. In just three hours, the initiative raised $153 million, more than 50 percent more than its initial goal.

A startup company backs several of the cryptocurrencies that hit the market. This company created the blockchain that tracks the coins for a specific reason, whether it's to make it easier to transmit money across borders, improve supply chain tracking, or provide some other feature that businesses and consumers would find appealing. The company will conduct an initial coin offering to collect funds for the initiatives and to boost the cryptocurrency's appeal (ICO). In some aspects, these are similar to an initial public offering (IPO), in which a firm raises funds by selling stock. However, there are significant distinctions between an IPO and an ICO.

When you invest in an ICO, you're buying the cryptocurrency that the blockchain company is selling. This does not entitle you to a share of the company's ownership. You don't get a say in how Ripple works just because you hold XRP. You do not have a say in Ethereum's next upgrade if you buy ether. Instead, you simply purchase the money and determine when you want to sell it.

This is not the same as an initial public offering (IPO). You do receive a vote if you hold stock in a public corporation. You have thirty votes if you own thirty shares. While this does not grant you decision-making authority within a Fortune 1,000 company, it does offer you some control over how your investment functions. It also offers some investor safeguards, such as remedies if the corporation engages in dishonest behavior.

Since they've become a popular tool to defraud investors, ICOs have become a renowned microcosm of the crypto investing experience. This has led to a lot of criticism of the ICO regulations because organizations who release the coins don't have to offer much information about how they function, what growth strategy they have, or what goals they have for the future. They are not required to divulge their balance sheets, produce proof of a sale, or disclose earnings data. In essence, these companies are nothing more than phantoms beyond the information they choose to provide with potential coin buyers on their own.

When you invest in an IPO, this is not the case. Companies are obliged to present thorough financial information to the SEC before the IPO's launch. This information is made public prior to the IPO date, allowing potential investors to assess the company's health.

Companies that launch initial coin offerings (ICOs) are typically small and new. They lack a long track record of performance, years of earnings, or even a large number of investors (although some do have an angel or series-A investors).

An IPO often occurs when a firm has demonstrated its potential to expand revenues or profits over a period of time. Because the company's financial data will be made public during the IPO process, institutional and retail investors will assess the company's performance, delivering a severe assessment of where it has been and where it is headed. This eliminates companies that have no legitimate purpose to go public other than to make a quick buck. During the ICO process, it's more challenging to spot these fraudulent actors.

The appeal of investing in ICOs stems from the ability to buy into a new coin for a meager price, allowing you to possess a more significant stake in the company. The other reason is this: Bragging rights for getting a head start on a coin that takes off. Both of these are excellent reasons to buy an ICO domain name. Just keep in mind that if you select this path, there's a good chance the money you spend will never be seen again.

The quantity of shares you can obtain in a currency if you buy it from the beginning is the reason you buy into an ICO. You would have roughly seventy-four coins if you purchased $100 in the ether in September 2015. That would be roughly nine coins if you did the same thing in September 2016. Is it still the same in 2017? Approximately one-quarter of a coin by the end of 2017, the early investor would have profited almost $53,000, while the person with nine shares would still have a healthy $6,500, and the late investor would have more than doubled his initial $100 investment. If you're correct, being early certainly pays off.

ICOs have been the most common way for new coins to enter the cryptocurrency market as the sector has increased in popularity, but they aren't the only way. Expect more solutions to be launched as technology advances and organizations become more aware of the possibilities of cryptos. This will provide a whole new approach to monitoring prospective future players in the game. Consider these three alternate ways to obtain coins for the time being.

Initial Coin Offerings (ICOs), also known as "token sales" or "token generation events," is a novel way for businesses to acquire funds without diluting their ownership or needing to repay investors. ICOs are a hybrid of traditional fundraising methods with a few twists, and the term 'ICO' appears to have been coined (ha) to connote IPOs or first public offerings of stock. According to icodata.io, 220 billion dollars was raised through some sort of ICO between 2014 and mid-2018. Mastercoin (July 2013) and Maidsafe (July 2014) were early ICOs, but they used the term 'crowd-sale.' In 2017, initial coin offerings (ICOs) became popular.

A corporation can traditionally generate funds in one of three ways: equity, loans, or pre-ordering specific products. They can raise money from a small group of investors, as is common in early venture capital, or from a vast number of people, a method known as 'crowdfunding,' which is becoming more popular.

In an equity raising, investors pay money to the company in exchange for a piece of the company's ownership. Among other benefits, investors receive a share of the company's profits in the form of dividends and may have voting rights at shareholder meetings. Investors lend money to the company in a debt raising and may get periodic interest payments in the form of coupons. Debtors anticipate receiving their money back at the end of the loan's term. Consumers (note that they are customers, not investors) pay money for a product that will be delivered later in a pre-fund or pre-order. The product is frequently not yet ready for distribution. Early ordering might sometimes result in a discount.

Crowdfunding is a relatively new phenomenon that takes advantage of the internet's potential to allow a project or company to be funded by soliciting small sums of money from a large number of people, usually through a web or app-based platform that connects projects with investors or customers. The 'crowd' can be used to raise any form of finance. Seedrs, AngelList, CircleUp, and Fundable are examples of equity crowdfunding sites. Prosper, Lending Club, and Funding Circle are examples of debt crowdfunding platforms. These services are also known as 'peer to peer lending platforms. Kickstarter and Indegogo are two pre-funding platforms that work on a pledge basis, meaning that a project only moves forward if a particular amount of money is donated. This is common for products that cater to a specific market. Pre-ordering is expected in the book and video game industries.

In a document known as a whitepaper, companies221 define a specific product or service and announce their ICO. Investors222 pay money to the firm in the form of cryptocurrency in exchange for tokens or a promise of tokens in the future. The tokens can represent anything, but they are most commonly used to represent financial assets tied to the project's success (known as security tokens) or access to a product or service developed by the enterprise (and described as utility tokens). Tokens may be listed on one or more crypto-asset exchanges at some point. A product or service is eventually generated, and holders of utility tokens can redeem their tokens for the product or service.

Stages of ICO Funding

Private auctions. Investments, reductions, and bonuses are arranged individually between the project and each investor in private sales. The procedure is comparable to that of a traditional startup seeking angel or seed capital.

A contract that describes the legal agreement between the project and the investor is frequently, but not always, present. The Simple Agreement for Future Tokens, or SAFT,228 is a common framework created and popularized by digital currency lawyer Marco Santori229 and others to promote industry self-regulation. The SAFT is a contract based on the Simple Agreement for Future Equity230, a popular startup template. A SAFT document is a contract that states that an investor will pay money now (in whatever form, fiat or cryptocurrency) in exchange for tokens at a later date. The SAFT is a sort of convertible note or a forward contract in general. Regardless of the token's classification, the SAFT is financial security in and of itself.

Public token sales. Those whose tokens may be categorized as securities are increasingly avoiding public token sales. However, because of their global reach, simplicity of financing, and hype-ability, they remain popular with some initiatives.

For receiving funds, the project typically generates an Ethereum smart contract231 and publishes the address on their website. In a process automated by the smart contract or a set of smart contracts, investors transfer money to the smart contract and receive tokens.

Tokens that are ERC-20 compatible and registered on the Ethereum blockchain may be used in some projects. Others, particularly companies developing new blockchain platforms, may first record tokens as ERC-20 tokens on Ethereum, which will be redeemed for tokens on the new blockchain once it is up and running.

Public auctions are usually well-publicized. Countdowns and widgets that reflect the amount raised are popular and are often prominently featured on the project's website. Public sales are advertised via social media, chat rooms, and bulletin boards.

Token pre-sale. Pre-sales are the "sale before the public sale," usually at a lower price per token or with bonuses offered to investors based on their investment level. They entice investors to invest at a lower cost and contribute to the enthusiasm around an ICO. An oversubscribed pre-sale serves as a potent psychological lure for investors in the primary public offering.

CHAPTER 13: ANALYSTS' EXPECTATIONS FOR THE CRYPTO MARKET IN THE NEXT DECADE

What is the future of cryptocurrencies? Within this space, it's the age-old question. It's also why investing in cryptos has such a high level of risk and volatility due to the absence of a clear answer. While prognosticators anticipate a plethora of possible outcomes, the only thing that is certain is that bitcoin is dependent on the blockchain. It depends not only on the growth of the blockchain but also on the necessity to incorporate specialized cryptos in order to provide its service. However, there is a universe where sophisticated cryptography isn't required. That world could appear in fifty years, five years, or never at all. There's no way of knowing.

The Evolution to Come

Many have compared the current condition of the blockchain to the dot-com boom of the 1990s. Given the current status of the blockchain, that may be a little premature. It's closer to the garage stage of development than the Silicon Valley level of acceptability in terms of utilization and viable businesses. However, the blockchain has been dubbed a "foundational technology," implying that it would not only disrupt the internet but will also build new platforms and applications that the world has yet to envisage.

What does this mean for bitcoin and other cryptocurrencies? It all relies on how tightly cryptos are tied to the blockchain. It's important to realize that while cryptocurrencies rely on the blockchain, the blockchain itself does not require cryptocurrencies—or even its own cryptocurrency—in order to work. The continual rise of cryptocurrencies as the constant currency within the blockchain will determine whether they progress beyond this early phase, where the coins act as the primary entrance point for investors and enthusiasts. The worst-case scenario for people investing in cryptocurrencies is for a government to create crypto that becomes the industry standard, as this suggests that the blockchain gamble, while exemplary, did not result in crypto wealth.

It's also a less likely situation today, given that blockchain founders appear to be enticed by the cryptocurrency funding model, which allows them to obtain funds without handing over control of their company to a venture capital firm.

Testing It Out

Businesses and governments are primarily just dipping their toes into the blockchain ecosystem at this stage. Financial institutions are experimenting with blockchain technology to see if it can handle cross-border transactions. Countries like Estonia are considering the use of blockchain to securely store information for various government organizations, where it serves as a hacker-proof digital storage file that is available 24 hours a day, seven days a week. The blockchain has been considered by hospitals as a means of securely storing medical records. This could theoretically be modified such that each person has their own living health record on a blockchain that doctors can access, providing them access to the patient's whole medical history in one place. These use cases have a lot of potential, but they haven't yet been shown to be successful. And they haven't created any viable enterprises to date.

Look for clear winners and losers to emerge from all of this testing in the future, similar to how Apple and Microsoft split from the rest of the computer companies back in the day, or how Google became the leading search engine or Facebook the dominating social media organization. The application of cryptocurrencies in these breaks will be determined by the company strategy, technology, and specific use case.

Blockchain is Everywhere

The early adoption of blockchain and cloud computing share certain commonalities. Companies wanted to market their use of cloud computing as it became a more powerful tool for storing large blocks of data, but most people didn't understand what a company meant when it said it would store your information "in the cloud." It became more of a buzzword, adding a lot of distractions to cloud computing, and some companies were just marketing services as a type of quasi-cloud storage, even if it had very little to do with storing information on independent servers.

Don't be shocked if you see more companies promoting the blockchain concept when the technology or use case has nothing to do with the blockchain. The idea of the blockchain has become a widespread phenomenon as a result of the success of cryptocurrencies, even if understanding of the blockchain remains quite a niche. While more people will presumably become familiar with this type of platform, don't be tricked into thinking that more mentions of the blockchain would result in a higher valuation for your coin, as many of these discussions may be superficial.

Consumers will eventually recognize when they are adopting existing blockchain technology, just as they have with the cloud. Similarly, with Amazon and Google in the consumer cloud market, a few companies will most likely step into the mainstream as the dominant suppliers.

Expect a Bursting Bubble

Valuations among this early set of creators will rise as technology advances, and new companies emerge that find momentum in the broader market. Many of these companies will become unicorns or startups valued at $1 billion or more if this technology has the legs that some believe it does. Some will be sold to much larger firms for millions to billions of dollars in initial public offerings, while others will be sold for millions to billions of dollars in sales to much larger firms. The price of blockchain companies will eventually reach unsustainable levels as belief in the technology reaches peaks similar to those observed in the cryptocurrency industry. The market will fall back once the euphoria hits these levels, similar to how the tech bubble burst in the late 1990s and early 2000s.

Optimism has led the crypto market since its mainstream entry, but that's to be anticipated. Rarely, if ever, is investing in a new tool and technology as simple as this. However, it will take even more enthusiasm to reach the heights to which many people believe it can soar. This will inevitably lead to a downturn, but in a booming industry, this is to be expected.

The blockchain will not be extinguished as a result of this. Instead, it will distinguish between legitimate enterprises and weaker businesses. A culling of the fat, like the introduction of a large number of cryptocurrencies, isn't always a terrible thing. It will cause some suffering in the short term, but the blockchain world will be a better place as a result. It is hoped that it would help bring stability to the crypto markets.

How Technology Needs to Develop

There are a few difficulties that firms are attempting to resolve in order for cryptocurrencies to have a seat at the table as the blockchain continues to advance. These characteristics will be critical for the development of cryptos. While solutions have already emerged, if individual cryptocurrencies are to continue to function as the primary tools for transacting on the blockchain, numerous rounds of repairs will be required before they are set in stone.

Cryptocurrency Scaling

There is a massive issue with scale, which refers to the ability of a cryptocurrency to grow in size without sacrificing transaction speed or liquidity. Bitcoin and ether, the most popular cryptos, only process a few transactions per second. It poses a significant difficulty for cryptos, as they must compete with conventional processors in order to become more widespread. Visa is capable of processing over 55,000 transactions per second, but on average, only handles about 2,000. Even though it may go considerably faster, PayPal averages roughly 200 transactions per second. If cryptocurrencies want to compete for the types of customers that Visa, Mastercard, PayPal, and others cater to, they will have to address this issue head-on.

Privacy of Using the Coins

The transactional history of Bitcoin is stored on the blockchain, ready to be downloaded by anyone who wants to look at it. There is nothing that precludes someone from following a coin's spending history (even if it would be challenging to do). It's one of the reasons why businesses are afraid to use the coin on a larger scale, among other things. Instead, if a company accepts bitcoins, the coins are usually cashed out right away. This not only locks in a set price, but also inhibits them from spending bitcoin for other purposes, such as purchasing company supplies. Why wouldn't they want to do that using bitcoin?

Even if it takes time to identify the person or entity making the purchase, most businesses do not desire a public record of all of their transactions. The larger the company, with more competitors, investors, followers, critics, and journalists, the more it will want to keep practically all of its transactions hidden as much as possible. They will not want to trade on a public blockchain.

Ethereum has taken moves to make transactions more private, which will encourage commercial clients to adopt it more. Other cryptos have also implemented more secure options. But, with these remote possibilities, these coins will have to combat the acceptance of the currencies for more sinister purposes, including on the black market. The more private these coins become, the more probable they will be adopted by a criminal subculture. The purpose is to establish a secure environment for privacy.

They Must Overcome Threats from the Government

Cryptocurrencies piqued the interest of anti-government activists because they offered an alternative to fiat currency, which is controlled by a central bank. For the general public, however, having the dollar as the principal means of conducting business or transacting has appeal. It'ssimple: knowing the money is secure, functional, and not in danger of becoming obsolete is comforting.

For all of these cryptocurrencies to exist, they must continue to offer a benefit that the fiat currency cannot match. That benefit is currently the use of the currency in the digital realm. However, if a significant fiat currency, such as the US dollar, wanted to create a cryptocurrency version of itself, there's no reason why it wouldn't become the most widely accepted cryptocurrency. Companies would seek blockchain companies to provide solutions that would allow them to accept the dollar cryptocurrency. And if the dollar crypto gained enough traction, it would swiftly become the most widely acknowledged cryptocurrency.

It's unlikely that blockchain companies would embrace it right now, given that cryptocurrency has been the source of the majority of their profits in the industry thus far. However, if blockchain companies grow to be billion-dollar corporations, this could alter. The value of the company will then appear to be as appealing — if not more so — than the specific cryptocurrency. Would they accede to these demands? It's entirely plausible, which is why these cryptos will need to continue changing, adapting, and growing to compete with fiat currencies. Acceptance by the general public is a big part of it. The other aspect has to do with technological advancements.

Legal Clarity Will Help

In the crypto market, trading the news isn't a profitable strategy, but it's understandable why investors are concerned when another government takes a hard stance against cryptocurrency. With such a new industry, there's no guarantee that this technology will continue, which makes an investor worried if another government decides it's not a solution that should be allowed to thrive within the country's borders. From a mainstream standpoint, the development of regulations around cryptocurrencies—with a clear definition of what is and isn't legal—will undoubtedly result in a higher capacity to trust the tools.

If, on the other hand, regulations continue to change according to the whims of particular leaders, cryptocurrencies will struggle to gain traction since another restrictive law will suffocate any upward momentum. These guidelines are constantly being developed, and none have been put in stone. Hopefully, some clarity will emerge shortly.

Smart Safety Measures

As a believer in cryptos and a coin investor, what you want to see from a legal aspect are measures that make trading and transacting with the coins considerably safer. Restrictions on exchanges and developers to encourage more robust security will enable for better understanding, study, and implementation of the currency. For this reason, you do not want to discourage legal limitations on currencies. You only want the constraints to do with securing your investment rather than completely restricting it.

Options for All

Currently, cryptocurrencies are only used in a few fields. It's all about spending bitcoin for mainstream people. Ethereum, Ripple, Stellar, or another up-and-coming altcoin may be used by businesses, depending on their goals. For the time being, Ripple is attracting banks, while Ethereum appears to be a viable development alternative. Despite this, there hasn't been a cryptocurrency that can be used for all of these uses. It's also why, in terms of both valuation and technology, no single cryptocurrency stands out. (Keep in mind that bitcoin is the technology underpinning many of the altcoins that were created to improve on the original idea.)

Whether or whether one cryptocurrency will one day stand out from the crowd will be determined by how adaptable it is to various situations, technology (such as blockchains), and goals.

What Happens If This Currency Is Created?

Let's pretend that one coin is the only one in the market. Ultimatecoin has become the recognized coin for all blockchain companies, mainstream users, and businesses and is dubbed ultimatecoin. It's the only one who has made it. While this situation may appear far-fetched at this time, it is possible.

If this happens, ultimatecoin will trade like other fiat currencies, with tiny fluctuations over time influenced by inflation or demand, depending on whether the coin has a maximum quantity of coins available.

If you buy in this form of cryptocurrency early on, you will be rewarded handsomely, as it will have to gain considerable value before reaching this level. Aside from that, it won't be a fascinating investment because once it reaches a level of consistency, it won't move much.

What Happens If There Isn't Any Such Currency?

By looking at the current market, you may argue that this appears to be the most probable situation. Instead, crypto coins will become more like equities in that they will be solid coinage with a documented track record. Meanwhile, new coins will emerge with legitimate purposes and use-cases, addressing issues that the current market is unable to address.

As they'll be dependent on a high level of adoption in this situation, these coins will continue to offer fluctuating returns. Even if the acceptance is granted, the market will be divided, with daily volatility that will frighten some investors. However, you may picture a few coins demonstrating constancy in this situation, indicating that they will be the portfolio's stalwarts, while others opt to bet on newer names.

The good news is that as the market develops in this direction, the use of phony ICOs will decrease. Weak coins or technology will not mislead the market as readily, especially when best practices emerge, and organizations adjust to filter out unscrupulous players before they acquire popularity.

If the Funds Have Been Approved

It's not as if you'd want to leap into the market right away if your finances were approved. To be sure the funds are worth the money; you'll want to look at a few details about them first. These would include the following:

- Fees: You don't want overly high fees to eat up all of your gains.
- Cryptocurrencies: What does the ETF or index fund invest in? You want to be able to access a large portion of the crypto market.
- Active management: Who makes the decisions on where the money is spent? An index fund connected to the scale of the crypto industry is a better bet.

It's crucial to keep in mind that just because you have access to a fund like this doesn't mean you're diversified. Because so many coins trade alongside bitcoin, there's little proof that the crypto ecosystem is diverse. Instead, you've increased your exposure to a more considerable number of names in the crypto market, capturing those that begin to rise or break through the bitcoin ceiling.

If the crypto market becomes more prominent, the SEC may be forced to accept these funds in the future. It helps that more traditional financial businesses are showing interest, but whether the government will start to take the market seriously is still unknown.

The Long-term Hope

The reason you put your additional investing cash into cryptocurrencies is to see where they go from here. The options are still wide open. Could they become a global currency that can be used to transact in financial markets all over the world? Will they be consigned to the outskirts of the digital marketplace, staying a specialized purchasing tool? The most likely scenario is somewhere in the middle.

However, you want to see those transaction rates increase. The most incredible comfort—and eventual stability—in the marketplace will come from seeing organizations really use the tools to do big-sized business, which will lessen the volatility of your investment. It will also lead to rises that aren't inconsistent or bubble-like but rather reflect a long-term value in the purpose and technology that reflects the digital age's evolution.

And what if it does become the world's global currency? You'll be glad you were able to get in when you did.

INVESTING
IN
NFTS

CHAPTER 14:
WHAT ARE NFTS: MEANING

An NFT is, in essence, a collectible digital asset, which holds value as a form of cryptocurrency. Much like art is seen as a value-holding investment, now so are NFTs. NFT stands for non-fungible token – a Digitaltoken thatis a type of cryptocurrency, much like Bitcoin or Ethereum. But unlike a standard coin in the Bitcoin blockchain, an NFT is unique and cannot be exchanged like-for-like (hence, non-fungible). To reiterate, this kind of token is like Bitcoin, except while you can trade Bitcoin and have more of the same thing that represents real moneyat a varyingmarketvalue, each NFT is unique.

So, what makes an NFT more special than a run-of-the-mill crypto coin? Well, the file stores extra information, which elevates it above pure currency and brings it into the realm of, well, anything, really. The types of NFTs are super-varied, but they could take the form of a piece of digital art or a music file – anything unique that could be stored digitally and be thought of to hold value.

Essentially, they are like any other physical collector's item, but instead of receiving an oil painting on canvas to hang on your wall, for example, you get a JPG file.

You possess the token that says you own something, like an art piece, and you can trade it, but if you do, you'll be getting an entirely different piece. To keep all the parts in place, there's enforced (artificial, but isn't everything?) scarcity.

It's easy enough to wrap your head around the fact that a piece of art can be created and exist on a screen, beityourphone, computer, tablet, etc.

Then, that piece of art can be seen, screen-shotted, and downloaded by anyone online. But the deeper concept of NFT art is agreed-upon value and ownership; even if anyone can see, download, print out and hang up a piece of digital art, only a select few can actually own that exact piece. So NFTs is a form of digital asset, whose ownership is recorded on a blockchain.

CHAPTER 15:
DIFFERENT TYPES OF NFTS

Significant topics of discussion involve the different conjectures regarding the NFT potential, and the value and risks associated with them. The true origin of an asset with the functionalities of blockchain could be explained by NFTs. Holding, limiting, or rejecting access to the rights of a person could be helped by NFTs, thereby guaranteeing exclusiveness. The applications of NFTs could be nurtured in various sectors by the development in the infrastructure and an increased opportunity for novelty in the NFTs space. Therefore, new types of NFTs can be reasonably expected to emerge. You can look at some of the notable NFT types which are popular in present times. The protuberant records in a nonfungible tokens list would include the following,

- Collectibles
- Artwork
- Event tickets
- Music and media
- Gaming
- Virtual items
- Real-world assets
- Identity
- Memes
- Domain names

An overview of these different nonfungible tokens or NFT variants to understand their significance is given below.

Collectibles

With the development of Cryptokitties the leading example of NFTs, the collectibles emerged. As a point of fact, the first occurrence of people using NFTs are Cryptokitties. As a matter of interest, Cryptokitties became popular enough in 2017 to congest the Ethereum network. One of the conspicuous accompaniments to the non-fungible tokens list in the class of digital collectibles is Cryptokitties. They are fundamentally digital kittens with discrete traits that make them prevalent and promising than others.

Artwork

Another projecting contender for NFTs is the artwork. The usual non-fungible tokens in this area mention programmable art, containing an exceptional blend of creativity and technology. As of now, many limited-edition artwork pieces are in circulation with the scope for programmability under certain conditions. To create images represented on blockchain networks oracles and smart contracts could be used by artists, which could help greatly. Participation from the legacy arts industry has also been stimulated by NFTs. The adoption of NFTs could be encouraged by the tokenization of real-world assets. The interesting prospects for scanning a code or sticker on assets could be offered by the possibilities of combining blockchain and IoT together. The NFT types in artwork could certify that ownership of real-world artwork on a blockchain network could be easily registered. Successively, the complete history of an artwork, such as previous ownerships and the prices for which they were sold in the past could be found by users.

Event Tickets

Event tickets are another promising addition among the types of NFTs. Attending events like music festivals and concerts are allowed to verify their identity and tickets using such types of NFTs. A specific number of NFT tickets could be mined on a selected blockchain platform by the event managers. Customers could buy the tickets through an auction and those tickets could be stored in their wallets easily accessible through mobile devices.

Music and Media

The domain of music and media leads to another category of NFTs due to the experiments they are trying to carry out with NFTs. Music and media files could possibly be linked to NFTs, enabling an individual with true ownership claim to access the files. The two noticeable platforms helping artists in minting their songs as NFTs include Rarible and Mintbase. The listeners get a quality experience while the artists get the benefits of reaching out directly to their followers and new audience. One of the leading reasons for infusing traits of vintage vinyl records is the intellect of uniqueness in purchasing NFT music. Consistent projections for addressing the concerns of music piracy and intermediaries could be offered by the growth of music NFTs in the non-fungible tokens list.

Gaming

In the domain of gaming, the common types of non-fungible tokens are principally fixated on in-game items. Profound levels of interest have been aroused among game developers by NFTs. NFTs could provide the functionality of in-game item ownership records, accelerating the growth of in-game economies. Most importantly, NFTs in the gaming segment also focus on announcing a wide display of benefits for players. While in-game collectibles were mutual necessities for a better gaming experience, NFTs have the prospective for changing their value Money could be easily recovered by in-game items as NFTs by selling it outside the game. On the flip side, game developers or the creators allotting NFTs could receive a royalty for every sale of items in the open marketplace.

Real-world Assets

Many NFT types could not be found serving as tokens for real-world items, it could be possible due to the progress in the NFT domain. For instance, right now many NFT projects are concentrating on the tokenization of real estate alongside luxury goods. NFTs are fundamentally deeds, that can familiarize the flexibility for buying a car or home with an NFT deed. Consequently, NFTs demonstrating real-world assets can capitalize on the prospects with cryptographic proof of ownership.

Identity

Non-fungible tokens have a critical trait and that is a rarity. Every NFT is unique and cannot be substituted with any other token. The working of identity NFTs is similar to that of event tickets NFTs. They can function as unique identifiers, hence aiding as trustworthy sustenance for the identity management systems. The commonly used applications of identity-based NFTs are unmistakable in certifications and licensing. The identity management sector for proving and verifying records of an individual could be changed by minting certifications and licenses and NFTs. Furthermore, identity-based NFTs could also make certain that individuals could store proof of their identity without risking losing it.

Memes

The most noteworthy development in the domain of NFTs recently is the sale of memes as NFTs. While being a fragment of widespread culture and a favorite among internet users, memes have also been related to NFTs. Selling the memes as NFTS displays the prospective for unique meme creators to participate in a progressing revolutionary ecosystem.

Domain Names

Domain names are another category of NFTs which have become popular recently. The top examples of domain name NFTs are Decentralized Domain Name Services such as Unstoppable Domains and the Ethereum Name Service (ENS). ENS aids in translating long and complex user addresses to a flexible and friendly experience for users with easier onboarding. The prevailing admittances in the non-fungible tokens list clearly portray the potential that the NFT ecosystem possesses. It is said to be a new class of digital or tokenized assets, NFTs are altering the predictable concepts of asset usage and ownership.

Consequently, you can find the common types of non-fungible tokens concentrating on what you get with an NFT. Firstly, you can have an original NFT created and stored on the blockchain. The second type of NFTs denotes digital natives in which numerous NFTs serve as parts of ownership rights to specific assets. The third category of NFTs only proposes access to NFT metadata, permitting you to use the NFT rather than distribute ownership. The various kinds of NFTs that are being distributed such as artwork, music, and media, domain names, memes, also demonstrate capable prospects for the future of NFTs.

CHAPTER 16: INVESTMENT GUIDE:GETTING STARTED

Do Your Homework

There's a reason this is number one. It is your obligation to conduct enough research regarding the companies, coins, services, and other entities with which you are investing in cryptocurrencies or purchasing NFTs. Sorry for being so 'mum' about it, but this is your money, and it deserves to be taken seriously. As a result, take your time and conduct as much research as you believe is necessary. Also, don't rely on a just one source of information.

Do Not Take Everything You See on social media At Face Value.

We adore social media, and we adore most of the people we meet there. But...there are folks on there who have their own agendas, and those agendas aren't always to assist you out. It's to take advantage of other people's ignorance and scaremonger for personal gain. There are certainly a lot of folks there who have good intentions but are simply misguided. In fact, the category of well-intentioned people vastly outnumbers the fraudsters, but even those who wish to help don't always have all the information. So, if you come across something that sounds interesting, strange, or incorrect, go back to step 1 and conduct your own investigation.

Don't Give Out Your Keys, Passwords, Or Bank Account Information.

Isn't it simple? Surely, it's self-evident? No, not if you're new to crypto and NFTs, which is what a lot of people are hoping for. If you're not familiar with the language (pro tip: check out our crypto dictionary for an overview of common words), someone asking for your private key (which is unique to you and should never be shared!) to arrange a bitcoin or NFT transfer may seem quite normal. It's not the case. Stop and check things out if somebody asks for information from you, especially if it comes out of nowhere. Some information can be provided, but your private key, banking information, login information, or anything else should never be, and if something seems fishy, be merciless and reject until you can check more. (Hint: if someone is pressuring you to provide information for a 'limited time offer,' it's probably a fraud.)

Always Remember the Old Proverb, "If It Looks Too Good to Be True, It Generally Is."

Scammers rely on people's desire for excellent offers and their inability to investigate them. Make sure you're not one of them. A fair amount of skepticism is the best defense. If an offer appears that appears to be too good to be true, investigate it. Ask people in your local community groups whether they've received similar offers or if they know anything about the person or corporation making the offer. It's quite acceptable to be cautious.

Participate In Crypto Communities.

It's quite beneficial to have a network of people who have already been there and done that, especially when you're just getting started. If you're new to crypto and NFTs, it's a good idea to join a few online communities to get advice, learn more about the industry, and have some fun. As previously said, these can be useful resources for gathering information and double-checking assumptions and interesting and enjoyable locations to communicate with like-minded people. Terra Virtua has a Discord server and a Telegram channel, both of which are full of amazing people who are always willing to share their knowledge. You may also keep up with NFT news and developments by following us on Twitter, Instagram, and Facebook.

Don't Put More Money into Something Than You Can Afford to Lose.

This, along with the phrase "previous performance is no guarantee of future results," is common investment advice. Both are important to keep in mind if you decide to invest in crypto or NFTs. Because cryptocurrency is such a volatile market, everything can change on a dime. And no matter how much people pretend to know what is a "sure bet," the truth is that no one knows for sure. If you are not comfortable with that degree or level of risk, it may not be an ideal investment for you.

Check and Double-Check the Information of Anyone or Company Who Approaches You.

This one may seem like a rehash of the last two, and it is, but it is so crucial that we don't mind repeating it. If anyone approaches you with an offer, whether it's an individual or a firm, go back to step one and DO YOUR RESEARCH. It's understandable if it sounds like common sense. But, because we all know how exciting and fast-paced the crypto world is, it's easy to get caught up in all the excitement. We'll give you one last piece of advice: don't haste! Cryptocurrencies and NFTs aren't going away, so don't feel compelled to participate by friends or the media if you're not ready.

CHAPTER 17:
INVESTING IN NFTS:
ADVANTAGES AND
DISADVANTAGES

Presently, NFTs have their advantages and disadvantages like any innovation, and in this segment, the accompanying can be featured

Advantages

They permit us to address computerized and genuine items in an interesting and unrepeatable manner inside the Blockchain. So, we can utilize this innovation to deal with these topics securely consistently. Would you like to tokenize your home or your vehicle utilizing an NFT? You can do it; now, your creative mind is the cutoff.

The advancement prospects of NFTs are perpetual; anything that you can address carefully can turn into an NFT. For instance, space names (those used to distinguish website pages) can be addressed as an NFT inside a DNS on the Blockchain. Here is the thing that occurs with the Namecoin project and the Ethereum Name Service.

The production of NFT can be adjusted to any blockchain, and it tends to be executed in an extremely secure manner. A model is Bitcoin, which with its restricted programming limit can address NFTs, keeping the security hazards for such resources for a base, it figures out how to address NFTs.

The presence of norms makes their creation, execution, and advancement simpler.

Opportunities for cross-chain interoperability with tasks like Polkadot or Cosmos.

Disadvantages

While there are norms for creating NFT, they are not dependable nor complete as far as usefulness. The previously mentioned is the primary motivation behind why, for instance, the ERC-721 badge of Ethereum (the most utilized for NFT in Ethereum) tries to be supplanted by the ERC-1155 token, which is significantly more secure and has new capacities.

NFTs are overseen by complex shrewd agreements, making their tasks mind-boggling and weighty (as far as data). These two things raise the estimation of the commissions that should be paid to complete exchanges. So, running NFT can be costly, particularly if the organization is blocked and commissions soar.

Like Defi, NFT stages are more defenseless to hacks since everything is taken care of by brilliant agreements and different interfaces to control them. This whole layer of programming adds assault vectors that programmers can misuse for malignant increase.

CHAPTER 18: MARKETPLACE FOR NFT

Non-fungible tokens (NFTs) had been existing for a long, but it wasn't until 2021 that they were widely known. The cryptographically unique tokens represent a title of ownership over the digital property such as music, videos, or art—but it was the digital art scene that ignited the NFT market, with headline-grabbing sales like Beeple's $69 million Christie's auction grabbing global attention.

Since then, fans have leapt on every new NFT fad, spending hundreds of dollars (if not millions) on games like CryptoPunks, Bored Apes, and Loot. However, you might be asking where you can get these NFTs. NFT marketplaces have sprung up like a thriving virtual high street, selling digital art and collectibles at all price points. Some of the most known platforms are listed below.

Axie Marketplace

The NFT-powered video game Axie Infinity hosts the second largest NFT marketplace, with a cumulative trade volume of higher than $2.1 billion on Dappradar. It solely deals in Axies, cute Pokémon-style digital critters that players may purchase and sell on the Axie Marketplace.

You can also make new Axies using the game's built-in breeding mechanics, which you can then sell on the Marketplace. Unlike art NFTs, which are acquired solely for the purpose of collection, The NFTs in Axie Infinity have a purpose: they may be used in-game to combat monsters and other players, earning tokens that can be utilized to produce new species. The NFTs developed by

Axie Infinity has proven to be so lucrative that some players in the Philippines and Indonesia make a life breeding and trading them.

For novice users, Axie Infinity is one of the most difficult NFT services to use, and you will have to pass a few hurdles before you can even begin playing.

You will need to set up a Ronin wallet, transfer ETH into Ronin, and buy at least three Axies on the Axie market in addition to an Ethereum wallet like MetaMask (which will set you back several hundred dollars). This is not ideal for casual passers-by, but it's not beyond a seasoned crypto user's capabilities.

OpenSea

The world's first and largest peer-to-peer NFT marketplace is OpenSea. It has an overall transaction volume of over $6.5 billion at the time of writing, according to analytics platform DappRadar, enabling NFTs of everything from in-game collectibles and items to music, GIFs, artwork, and more.

The simplest way to sign up is to connect your MetaMask wallet, however alternative wallets like Bitski, Coinbase Wallet, Formatic, and others are also supported.

Purchasing an NFT is a simple process after you've connected; you only need to browse through the various collections, search for something that catches your attention, then submit an offer and wait to see if it is approved.

Uploading your own NFT work is so simple. Just go to the "Create" tab, then connect your wallet as a creator, and upload your NFT, complete the description, and stand by or wait for the millions to pour in.

Larva Labs/CryptoPunks

CryptoPunks was one of the first NFT demonstrations on the Ethereum network, a sequence of 10,000 randomly produced characters with a pixel art look and different features. While they were originally freely available, they are now only available for purchase.

What Do CryptoPunks Do and What Are They? Ethereum's NFT Sensation

The market for crypto collectibles exploded once non-fungible tokens (NFTs) became widespread in 2021, with $2.5 billion in transaction activity in the first six months.

This entails visiting CryptoPunks founder Larva Labs' marketplace, where the majority of sales are made. The cheapest Punk presently costs 94.99 ETH (approximately $285,000), while the most valuable one (number 3100) sold for a staggering $7.58 million. That explains Larva Labs' total trading volume of $1.3 billion. To begin, connect your MetaMask wallet, browse the available Punks (those with red backgrounds are for sale), and place your bid. The most difficult aspect of the operation is convincing yourself to spend such a significant lot of money, but that's entirely up to you. After all, the observer determines the value of art.

Rarible

Rarible is a community-run website that sells a variety of digital art and collectibles. It's one of Ethereum's most popular NFT exchanges. It currently has the fifth-highest all-time trading volume, according to Dappradar, with $210 million changing hands.

Just like on OpenSea, you can buy and sell any type of material. Sellers can also create several NFTs for a single image to sell it more than once.

The user interface of Rarible, which is simple enough for relative crypto rookies to operate, will feel at home for those who have dabbled in similar NFT marketplaces like OpenSea.

You can log in with MetaMask, Coinbase Wallet, MyEtherWallet, or any other WalletConnect-compatible mobile wallet. After you've signed up, you can use funds in your wallet to buy, or you can top up your wallet with fiat cash via bank transfer or debit card.

SuperRare

Compared to Rarible, SuperRare's UI is significantly more pared-back and straightforward, which overwhelms you with a bewildering array of flickering GIFs and live auctions.

It is also a lot more curated, as it describes itself as a social network dedicated to the creation and collection of crypto art. It works closely with artists, requiring submission and vetting of work before it can be offered, in other words, quality over quantity.

To sign up for SuperRare, you'll need a compatible wallet like MetaMask or Formatic. There is one more stage in which you must create a login and password that is tied to your wallet address, but it only takes a few seconds and you'll be browsing the platform's exclusive NFTs in no time.

KnownOrigin

KnownOrigin, like SuperRare, is committed to providing a more curated, gallery-like experience for the discerning NFT enthusiast. Its overall trade volume is less than $6.9 million. It stores all its artwork files on IPFS, which protects the underlying assets. Since this is a marketplace that avoids the wackier features of the NFT universe, there will be no charming monsters or wacky avatars will be found here.

NBA Top Shot Marketplace

NBA Top Shot is a compilation of digital trading cards based on NBA video highlights that were one of the first NFT series to gain traction with the general audience. When you purchase a pack, the clips are stored in your protected, encrypted blockchain-verified wallet, where you can view them or resell them on the NBA Top Shot Marketplace.

NBA Top Shot's popularity stems from the fact that its creators, Dapper Labs, made it simple for the average user to get started. To sign up for NBA Top Shot, simply link your Google account to Dapper, then input your phone number for SMS authentication.

Following that, you'll need to complete a few account-creation processes, including choosing your preferred team. After that, you can sign up for a fresh pack drop, which will put you in a virtual line to acquire one. After another verification from SMS, you can pay using an existing a Flow wallet, your Dapper money, crypto wallet, or, more conveniently, a credit card.

At the risk of sounding like a broken record, KnownOrigin is convenient to use. Simply connect your wallets, like MetaMask or Formatic, and you will be able to start bidding on your own NFT assets in no time.

6-Foundation

The Foundation, which touts itself as a "creative playground" for artists, has a total trading volume of slightly higher than $79 million at the moment. Nyan Cat's NFT, Edward Snowden's debut NFT, and an audiovisual digital collectible created by producer Richard D. James, best known as Aphex Twin, have all happened there.

Once you've connected your MetaMask or another software wallet to WalletConnect, you may access Foundation's marketplace with ease. On timed auctions, you can place bids exactly like you would on a regular auction site.

6-MakersPlace

MakersPlace is another specialized NFT marketplace that boasts a number of unique digital fine art collections. Despite its small size ($23.5 million at the time of writing), it features a number of one-of-a-kind objects that add to its exclusivity.

In February 2021, the site was taken down after famed crypto artist Beeple offered a collection of NFTs for $1 each. Shakira, T-Pain, and Rage Against the Machine's Tom Morello have all signed up for the website, which has hosted a number of NFT drops by performers.

Making an account on MakersPlace is straightforward, and you can save time by logging in with your Google or Facebook accounts.

You will need to choose five artists to follow as part of the registration process, and you will be able to buy their creations with either your MetaMask ETH balance or (more easily) your credit card. If you're a creator, you'll have to fill out an online form to request an invitation to join the platform, which the curators will assess.

The site features artists like The Weeknd, Grimes, and Eminem and a carefully curated collection of NFT releases that are released on a bi-weekly basis. It also has a marketplace where you may browse verified artists, curated collections, and a bigger selection of unconfirmed artists' work.

Getting started is a relatively simple procedure because of Nifty Gateway's direct connection with Gemini. To get started, you'll need to sign up for an account on the website (and use Stripe to authenticate your identity if you wish to sell NFTs). You will need to fund your account, either by sending ETH to a deposit address or with a credit card. After that, you are ready to purchase NFTs from the marketplace. You can connect your Gemini exchange account to your Nifty Gateway account, enabling you to make purchases as well as withdrawals using your Gemini exchange account balance (your Gemini account can be filled up using wire transfer, bank transfer, crypto deposits, and trades).

BakerySwap

BakerySwap is a smaller NFT exchange than OpenSea, which is understandable given that most NFT exchanges are based on Ethereum, whereas BakerySwap was one of the first to launch on Binance Smart Chain (BSC). The NFT marketplace, for example, is a feature of the site that allows users to trade and exchange liquidity assets directly with one another.

The NFT marketplace is easy enough to use, requiring only a MetaMask connection. NFT assets can only be obtained with BNB rather than the more commonly used ETH since this platform is based on the Binance Smart Chain.

Solanart

The most recent NFT mini boom took place on Solana, a competing blockchain to Ethereum. Collections like Degenerate

Ape Academy, SolPunks, and Aurory have seen trading volumes of hundreds of millions of dollars on platforms like Solanart. Unlike OpenSea, Solanart is a curated collection of NFT collections with a limited number of NFTs for sale. The NFT Revolution is underway.

Solana

Purchasing Solana NFTs with Phantom Wallet

August's NFT resurgence was dominated by Ethereum, the most popular blockchain network for crypto collectibles like CryptoPunks and Art Blocks. Despite the billions of dollars in trade activity, though...

To start buying Solana NFTs on Solanart, you'll need to download a Solana wallet like Solflare or Phantom and load it with Solana from your favorite exchange. Phantom features direct integration with the cryptocurrency exchange FTX, making it simple to deposit funds from that exchange.

It is as simple as going to your chosen NFT, connecting your Solana wallet to the marketplace, and then putting in your offer.

Binance NFT Exchange

Binance NFT marketplace is an NFT platform supplied by Binance, the world's largest crypto exchange, as you might think. To draw the exchange's enormous user base to its platform, the business plans to develop an NFT marketplace with exclusive collaborations and offers.

If you already have an account in Binance, you will be pleased to learn that it will automatically work with Binance NFT. After you've gotten in, all you must do is bid on any products that catch your eye. You can use ETH, BNB, or BUSD, depending on what the developers have listed.

CHAPTER 19:
HOW TO CREATE, BUY, AND SELL IN NFTS

NFTs have become one of the hottest crypto trends of 2021, with overall sales up 55% already since 2020, from $250 million to $389 million. Here's how you can create, purchase, and sell these popular digitals assets.

Non-fungible tokens (NFTs), which are unique collectible crypto assets, have been around as early as 2012 when the concept of Bitcoin Colored Coins first emerged. These coins were simply satoshis – small fractions of a bitcoin – marked, or "colored in" with distinct information that could link the coins to real-world assets, such as "this satoshi represents $500 of John Doe's New York office building." For the most part, however, Colored Coins were used to create and trade artwork like "Rare Pepe" digital cards on Counterparty, a peer-to-peer trading platform built on top of Bitcoin's blockchain.

These cartoon frog images adapted from a viral internet meme were some of the earliest examples of unique digital artwork tied to crypto tokens. This paved the way for the ideation and creation of new non-fungible token standards – a set of blockchain building blocks that allow developer to create their own NFT's.

NFTs can be used to represent virtually any type of real or intangible items, including: Virtual items within video games such as skins, virtual currency, weapons and avatars, Collectibles (e.g. digital trading cards), Tokenized real-world assets, from real estate and cars to racehorses and designer sneakers, virtual land**s, v**ideo footage of iconic sporting moments, etc.

How to create NFTs

Creating your own NFT artwork, whether it be a GIF or an image, is a relatively straightforward process and doesn't require extensive knowledge of the crypto industry. NFT artwork can also be used to create collectibles like sets of digital cards.

Before you start, you will need to decide on which blockchain you want to issue your NFTs. Ethereum is currently the leading blockchain service for NFT issuance. However, there is a range of other blockchains that are becoming increasingly popular, including:

- Binance Smart Chain
- Flow by Dapper Labs
- Tron
- EOS
- Polkadot
- Tezos
- Cosmos
- WAX

Each blockchain has its own separate NFT token standard, compatible wallet services, and marketplaces. For instance, if you create NFTs on top of the Binance Smart Chain, you will only be able to sell them on platforms that support Binance Smart Chain assets. This means you wouldn't be able to sell them on something like VIV3 – a Flow blockchain-based marketplace – or OpenSea which is an Ethereum-based NFT marketplace.

Since Ethereum has the largest NFT ecosystem, here's what you'll need to mint your own NFT artwork, music or video on the Ethereum blockchain:

An Ethereum wallet that supports ERC-721 (the Ethereum-based NFT token standard), such as MetaMask, Trust Wallet or Coinbase Wallet.

Around $50-$100 in ether (ETH). If you are using Coinbase's wallet you can buy ether from the platform with U.S. dollars, British pound sterling and other fiat currencies. Otherwise, you will need to purchase ether from a cryptocurrencyexchange.

Once you have these, there are a number of NFT-centric platforms that allow you to connect your wallet and upload your chosen image or file that you want to turn into an NFT.

The main Ethereum NFT marketplaces include:

- OpenSea
- Rarible
- Mintable

Makersplace also allows you to create your own NFTs, but you have to register to become a listed artist on the platform beforehand. OpenSea, Rarible and Mintable all have a "create" button in the top right corner.

Here's how the process works on OpenSea, currently the largest Ethereum-based NFT marketplace.

Clicking the "create" button (blue) will take you to a screen that asks you to connect your Ethereum-based wallet.

Once you've entered your wallet password when requested it will automatically connect your wallet with the marketplace.

You may have to digitally sign a message in your Ethereum wallet to prove you own the wallet address, but it'sjust a caseofclickingthroughtoproceed.

Digitally signing a message does not incur a fee, it's just to show that you have ownership over the wallet.

The next step on OpenSea is to hover over "create" in the top right corner and select "my collections." From there, click the blue "create" buttonasshown below.

A window will appear that allows you to upload your artwork, add a name and include a description. This part is essentially just you creating a folder for your newly createdNFT'sto go in.

Onceyou'veassigned an imageforyour collection, it will appear as shown below (blue). You'll then need to add a banner image to the page by clicking on the penciliconin the top right corner (red).

Now, you're ready to create your first NFT. Click on the "Add New Item" button (blue) andsign another message using your wallet.

You'll arrive at a new window where you can upload your NFT image, audio, GIF or 3D model.

On OpenSea and many othermarketplaces, you alsohave the optiontoincludespecial traits andattributes to increase the scarcity and uniquenessofyour NFT.

Creators even have the opportunity to include unlockable content that can only be viewed by the purchaser. This can be anything from passwords to access certain services to discount codes and contact information.

Once you 'refinished, click "create" at the bottom and sign another message in your wallet to confirm the creation of the NFT. The artwork should then appear in your collection.

Cost of Making NFTs

While it costs nothing to make NFTs on OpenSea, some platforms charge a fee. With Ethereum-based platforms, this fee is known as "gas." Ethereum gas is simply an amount of ether required to perform a certain function on the blockchain – in this instance, it would be adding a new NFT to the marketplace. The cost of gas varies depending on network congestion. The higher the number of people transacting value over the network at a given time, the higher the price of gas fees and vice versa.

Top tip: Ethereum gas fees are significantly cheaper on average during the weekend when fewer people are transacting value over the network. This can help keep costs down if you're listing multiple NFTs for sale.

How to sell NFT's

To sell your NFT on a marketplace, you'll need to locate them in your collection, click on them and find the "sell" button. Clicking this will take you to a pricing page where you can define the conditions of the sale including whether to run an auction or sell at a fixed price.

Etherand other ERC-20 tokens are the most common cryptocurrencies you can sell your NFT's for, however, some platforms only support the native token of the blockchain they were built upon. VIV3, for example, is a Flow blockchain market place and only accepts FLOW tokens.

By clicking on the "edit" button next to the collection image on OpenSea, signing the message using your wallet and scrolling down, you have the option to program in royalties and select which ERC-20 token you'd like to receive for selling the NFT. Royalties allow NFT creators to earn a commission every time the asset is sold to a new person. This has the potential to create lifelong passive income streams for artists and other content creators automatically thanks to smart contracts.

Listing NFT's on a marketplace sometimes requires a fee in order to complete the process. While it's not the case with every platform, it's something to be mindful of when creating NFT's.

How to buy NFT's

Before you rush to buy NFTs, there are four things you need to consider first:

- What market place do you intend to buy the NFTs from?
- What wallet do you need to download in order to connect with the platform and purchase NFTs?
- Which cryptocurrency do you need to fund the wallet with to complete the sale?
- Are the NFTs you want to buy being sold at a specific time, i.e. via a pack or art drop?

As you can probably guess by now, certain NFTs are only available on specific platforms. For example, if you want to purchase NBA Top Shot packs you will need to open an account with NBA Top Shot, create a Dapper wallet and fund it with either the USDC stablecoin or supported fiat currency options. You will also have to wait for one of the card pack drops to be announced and try your luck in trying to buy them before they sell out. Pack and art drops are becoming increasingly common as a method for selling scarce NFTs to an audience of hungry buyers. These drops normally require users to sign up and fund their accounts beforehand so that they don't miss out on the opportunity to purchase NFTs when they drop. Pack and art drops can be over in seconds, so you need tohaveeverythingreadyahead of time.

Where to buy NFT's

For cryptotraders who are primarily interested in buying NFTs, here is a list of the most popular NFT marketplaces in 2021:

- OpenSea
- Rarible
- SuperRare
- Nifty Gateway
- Foundation
- Axie Marketplace
- BakerySwap
- NFT ShowRoom
- VIV3
- Good Time To Get Into Non-Fungible Tokens

The NFT craze isfar from being over. Major brands and celebrities such as the UFC and Shawn Mendez have signed deals to release their own non-fungible assets soon, and even Elon Musk's girlfriend Grimes has jumped on the bandwagon selling almost $6 million worth of digital artwork in minutes. Messari analyst Mason Nystrom anticipates the NFT market will exceed $1.3 billion by the end of 2021 as more artists, brands and icons flock to the space to create their own distinctive tokens. With more blockchains competing to produce better NFT services too and a growing range of platforms to choose from, now is a great time to takepartin the space.

CHAPTER 20:
NFTS AS A CREATOR AND ARTIST

Buying and selling NFTs is one thing; there can be a lot of skill and know-how involved when predicting how the market works and how an item will turn. These are all the tools of an investor and a collector. But what's much different is trying to create your own NFT from your own original artwork or media. There is a significant amount of work to take up this practice and get your work out there, including stocks beyond that of just money and time.

So, when you're an artist, watching the millions of dollars being sold across the NFT market, you might find yourself a little left out, a little betrayed by the costs of entry in many of the different spheres that you'll find throughout the artist's world. This is a natural thought. NFTs give artists the chance to not only show their artwork to people across the world but earn a living while doing so. NFTs allow artists in digital art, music, and any form of multimedia to earn their worth and expand beyond the reaches of their works. NFTs are a creator's best friend.

Creatorship: The Basics to the Art

So, am I talking to you, or am I talking to the best artists out there? Am I talking to only the Beeples of the world, or am I talking to those who simply want to make money off their creations? The answer lies in exactly what you want out of your artwork. It lies in nearly anyone who has the skill to show the world one day and make a living off of making art. Any artist can make their art into an NFT; they just need to know where to start.

To start, you need to decide what level of complexity you would like to create your NFT under (Nepori, 2021). There are several different levels, and some might be easier than others, try and choose one that works best for you. The separate NFT complexities can be defined as the amount of coding required to mint the NFT on the blockchain market. There are many options that would be recommended as the easiest, that simply have you import a multimedia file into a third-party platform or marketplace, giving you the minting process easily and without hassle.

There are other ways that involve minimal amounts of coding, simply using APIs and other interfaces to help reduce the work required to set up a node on the blockchain. Then there is setting up your own node itself, which can only be recommended if you have significant knowledge in coding and already understand the blockchain system. Because this book is meant for beginners and these methods can involve many steps, just go with the easiest one for you and move on from there.

Next, because creating an NFT and hosting it on the blockchain comes at a price, we should fully understand what gas fees are and how they work.

As we have said before, gas fees are the operational costs of hosting an NFT or any other crypto token on the blockchain; however, how exactly does that affect you as a creator? Well, because creating can be a hard business in the first place, you might not have a significant amount of capital to be spending on gas fees, and the more you can avoid them, the better.

There are a couple of platforms that offer such a deal to do so. Platforms like OpenSea have a zero-gas fee option while other NFT marketplaces are beginning to emerge with similar concepts, like Immutable X and Mintable (OpenSea, 2021). Usually, though you might see them as completely free of gas prices, these platforms have a catch of some sort.

When looking out for gas-free options, ensure that you have fully researched the best option for you and your portfolio, or you might end up with the raw end of a deal.

Now that we know the cost of entry, it is probably time we took a look inside creating an NFT itself from scratch. This doesn't mean I will try and tell you how to create your art or anything like that. I will rather approach with different ideas that might help you cater your creations to the NFT market, giving you a better chance of selling your work. The first thing you'll want to do is narrow down what kind of NFT you would like to make, whether that be a piece of art, a game, or even a whole movie. Then, you'll want to decide on a standard for your NFT, which could be anything from ERC-721 to EIP-2309 and beyond; this is where your genre of NFT will matter as something unique and rich, like a movie, might sell better as a single item than say a doodle.

From here, you'll want to look at any trends in the market, fitting both your niche and your standard, and deciding on whether or not you wish to create something within that trend or not. After this, you'll likely start creating. The next process is finding the right marketplace to sell the item on, as some are better for specific items while others are better for more traffic. Once you've gone through posting the NFT on the marketplace, as a creator, it is recommended to keep track of that post and communicate around it, possibly creating your own social media websites, accounts, and even a Discord server for your buyers. This will not only allow you to closely track youritem but will inspire confidence in buyers who are looking at your product for growth. Once you've done all this, rinse and repeat. These fundamental elements are what you need to get started as a creator for an NFT but are just the first steps.

They will help you along the way into the world of NFT creatorship but cannot apply you to the niches you might need to understand or even the dedication you might need to give. To go beyond just selling one NFT to selling a whole brand of NFTs requires a massive overhaul of your methods with a focus on your specific area of expertise.

Let's give some advice on how to foster this deeper knowledge through different niches in the current or expanding markets.

Creatorship: Deeper Knowledge of the Craft

You might have one niche or several; however, you would probably agree that one of your chosen niches is better than another; you might make video shorts but focus yourself on the art aspect or the sound aspect. Once you select a niche you want to dive into, there is always the chance to go back and find another to explore, so don't feel like this is the end, but to create a brand in NFT, you must choose one specifically that you want to make your focus.

Once you've done this, you might be wondering what to do next. You might be wondering how you go from a focused niche to the brand names you see among the popular NFTs today. The answer lies in how one chooses to promote oneself as a creator and how each niche can best sell its product. So, now, let's explore some of the common art niches in the world and see how each one can go about promoting their art into a brand all their own.

The first niche is one you might expect, which is digital art. This niche is one that is thoroughly populated already, but with the growth of NFTs, there is always room for more. You can derive many of the best ways to promote your digital art from those who have gone before you. There are a plethora of different artists and groups of artists who have successfully made a brand out of their work. But how do you separate what works for them and what works for everyone else?

Well, there are some basic concepts that we've already gone over, like a social media presence or a well-constructed platform. Still, other than that, a few things can apply specifically to digital artists. Things such as rare drops, giveaways, or special showings all give your digital art and your NFT a better outlook.

Further from that, there is the trend of creating art NFTs that are simple, relatable, and similarly constructed, like that of CryptoPunks. These simple art pieces are not only very valuable on the market today but are instantly recognizable as the brand they're associated with. You, as a builder of a brand, want to make your work stand out from other NFTS, just like CryptoPunks, as the more people associate a specific trend of pieces with your work, the more they will know who you are and the more money they will pay to receive your pieces. This goes hand in hand with simply improving your work as an artist, and once you've sold a few NFTs, to begin with, you can go on to improve more, such as your software and your hardware.

All of this becomes possible once you've got the right tools, the right methods, and the right attitude to get the job done. A second niche that we've already seen many times, but haven't quite seen on the market is in music. This industry is rife with growth, but someone just has to pave the way. There are many things out there on the internet today that might help a music brand take off, including some that we've already mentioned in the paragraph on digital art. Drops, giveaways, and special events are always good for a brand as they are a service to the audience members who are there to support you, but with music, there can be quite a bit more. Because music can be a much more hands-on art niche, there might be quite a lot of interacting with fans on social media or even pitching your music to record labels who might make your music into an album, or possibly the creation of a whole website for your work— all of them a bit more apparent in music than in other niches.

Digital art, for example, does not often put on live concerts for their fans, and as such, the upkeep for a music-based NFT is more strenuous. But the rewards outweigh the costs. Websites, EPKs, and personal artist profiles can all be made with a bit of money and a little time, but the brand you'll be crafting out of them will live on to make much more.

Beyond music and digital art, there are a couple more niches that can benefit from the personal brand they can create through NFTs.

The next niche we'll look at is in the industry of video files and film. Unlike digital art and music, this niche cannot easily be done alone; however, if you are a group of people — or if you know a likely group of people —you can follow some of these different methods of creating a brand. The first thing that might come to mind when looking at film and video as NFTs are the NBA TopShot tokens that have recently made popular news. Though these highlights aren't necessarily film shots done artistically. They are rather done by professional directors working with a professional crew, and there is still quite a bit to be learned from them.

These small bites of a much larger meal can be replicated in a very similar way by even amateur directors and film crews, making their own interestingly new NFT. Now you might wonder how you are supposed to build a brand to rival that of the NBA, but you would be mistaken. These small clips can be thrown together and, because the market is nearly void of them at the moment, there is little need to create a brand for them. A quick introduction screen before the clip, whatever that content might be, sees a brand growing already. Combine that with a presence on social media, constant releases, and various other rewards, and you are well on your way to more sales.

The final niche that we will talk about is the video game industry that many have embraced over the last few years, as with Decentraland and The Sandbox. These games are, much like film and video, hard to get started as an individual but there is still much potential for them. Game assets, land, and other such items are very popular, but their work is well beyond the simple branding of a music creator.

Video games require a good interface, a well-designed world, and a fun concept to see the role of a brand even existing; however, if you were able to create a brand for a virtual world that you created, it would need a couple of things. Like all the other NFT brands, drops and giveaways will always help; however, there is a special focus on events that cannot be attributed to any of the other niches.

Because a brand of a video game includes the world of that video game itself, the assets and gameplay inside the game become especially important to spread awareness and attention to your brand. This means that the game's design is the most crucial measure of your video game brand, second to any sort of merch, drops, or giveaways that you might include as well. Always remember this.

Building a brand through any niche is a tough sell, and doing it successfully takes a lot of work and dedication, much like the work and commitment you might be used to putting into your craft. Once you begin to understand how each niche benefits and goes about making a brand, you'll realize that it can be done. And if it is done, there are for sure going to be rewards that you will reap in the sales and popularity of your products, and it is just the simple fact of getting started.

CHAPTER 21:
NFT REAL ESTATE

Virtual worlds have emerged as the child between video games and the internet, allowing us to interact with people online like we would in the real world. This gives us the chance to share, interact, and socialize with our friends and even random strangers we meet through these connections.

However, unlike the real world, these connections are monitored and controlled by the game company they are through. The expressions we make in sandbox games like Minecraft or Roblox, pieces of art that seem all our own, are actually just property of the centralized game company. These things we create are not ours in the grand scheme of things, even though they seem to be. This is where virtual real estate comes in.

Virtual real estate is the same idea as any video game like Minecraft or Roblox, with the capacity for creation, socialization, and expression, but is entirely owned by the users who make up its online world. This means that those who buy into these real estate opportunities will have a say in the overall world around them, giving players the power to create what they want to create and own it as they would own anything in the real world.

Platforms like Decentraland, The Sandbox, and Axie Infinity all present players with the choice to do what they like with the things they buy and own. This, as we will now see, is one of the newest and most revolutionary forms of NFT on the market today.

The Value in Digital Land and Property

Like any sort of cryptocurrency or currency in general, there is a distinct value that is based on two things: collective belief and transferability. Like most NFTs, virtual real estate represents a token that can be transferred much like a piece of land in the real world and can take on immediate value if sold. On the same level, virtual real estate is held valuable by the collective belief that it is valuable. This might be confusing to some, and we will explain each of these two concepts in more detail.

Collective belief is something that drives any piece of currency in the world, from the Euro to the USD; there is no intrinsic value in the piece of paper you are holding. Rather, there is extrinsic value in that the belief of everyone in the U.S or any other country believes that the USD is worth something, be that $1, $20, or $100. The difference is that intrinsic value is held inside the piece of paper itself. In contrast, extrinsic value is outside elements that make that piece of paper valuable, such as the U.Sgovernment. The same can be applied to virtual real estate. There is no intrinsic value to it, especially beyond theempty art assets that an empty parcel might take on, but there is extrinsic value to it.

The extrinsic value can be derived from the item's scarcity or simply the belief that it is worth something when it is within the finite set of other items. Because Decentraland, The Sandbox, and Axie Infinity all have only a certain amount of land to sell, there is value in that scarcity. People have been buying up that land to make their own even more valuable.

The transferability of virtual real estate can be a complex concept to grasp, as the idea of transferring a piece of land in the real world does not equate to 1:1 in the case of virtual real estate. There is no deed or any sort of document that you have to have to prove that you own that piece of land; rather ownership is represented by a smart contract.

This allows for easy movement — or transferability — of the asset from one person to another without having to jump through different hoops of deed and other government red tape. Additionally, the transferability of virtual real estate gives the market itself a boon in that investing in the land will be much easier than some REITs in the real world, basically with the same outlook on investment.

Virtual Real Estate: Platforms to Explore

Emerging from the news stories and articles about virtual real estate, there have been many different offshoots of platforms like Decentraland. Still, none have churned up quite the amount of attention as platforms like the original Decentraland, The Sandbox, or Axie Infinity. All of these different game worlds represent different styles of virtual worlds, allowing for investors and creators alike to make big money off of their investment into the unique world. Some of them are more focused than others, catering to specific niches of players, while some are open to almost any sort of player, creator, or investor. Let's explore each of these different lands in detail, highlighting ones that might be better suited for specific players.

The first platform we will talk about is Decentraland. This virtual world NFT is one of the largest of its kind, and every day it grows even larger – even as we speak, there are likely thousands of people online playing. More and more land is being taken up by investors, creators, and even artists who are looking to show off their work in revolutionary new galleries.

Recently an estate within the Decentraland virtual world sold for over $2.4 million, one of the largest sales of NFTs. It was bought by a fashion company looking to expand its ad coverage and advertise its brand through Decentraland's many different avenues.

But this is only the beginning. Many artists have now started buying up the token LAND in Decentraland to show off their art or digital art NFTs in galleries built by virtual creators, all supported inside the game itself with its easy-to-use building program. This blow-up is even then only one side of the story.

There are other sites within the Decentraland world that host things called scenes that can act as a whole new world for people who visit there. Players get the chance to create entirely new games within these small lots of LAND, while even allowing game creators to market the gaming experience to other players over the Decentraland world.

The process within Decentraland works much the same as any sort of sandbox game, like Minecraft or Roblox; however, without the centralized control, those game companies are allowed. This can be seen most clearly in the DAO, which is essentially the control structure for the game's world and the game itself.

The DAO is made up of token-holders who want to decide on the future of the game using a gas-less governance system, allowing the whole community of Decentraland to work to better the game as it sees fit. By this example, we can see exactly how Decentraland is one of the more popular decentralized virtual worlds.

The next platform that we will discuss is The Sandbox, which can be related to Decentraland; however, there are distinct differences that are worth mentioning. The first is the focus of the platform. With Decentraland, there is a lot of stock put on various things, from art showings to advertising to building and wearing custom assets.

With The Sandbox, there is a different focus on the actual gameplay involved in many of the games that have been created over the different parcels of land. It also has a more focused partnership with people like Atari games and Rollercoaster Tycoon, companies specializing in games. This virtual world can be more equated to a Ready Player One styled world with several different games jumbled together with avatars and custom design, all powered by owning three different NFTs called SAND, LAND, and ASSETS.

With these then, creators can make different experiences using the LAND of the world as a base for their games and ASSETs for the content of their game, then, as with Decentraland, the creators can charge for the game using SAND as the token of choice. It is also worth mentioning that SAND is the governance token for this world, allowing you to take part in the decisions of the world.

Besides buying and earning the required NFTs used in creating a game, there are options for game designers to earn a grant from what's called the Game Maker Fund, which strives to enrich the world of The Sandbox with well-designed games and experiences for its players. These, however, are just a few of the different benefits of investing in The Sandbox virtual world.

The last virtual world that has taken popular culture by storm has been Axie Infinity (Axie Infinity, 2021).This Pokemon-style game sees much of the same ideas as CryptoKitties but within a game all their own, allowing for battles, trading, breeding, all within the game world.

This idea has spread to the point that some of the rare lands in the virtual gaming world have sold for over $1.5million, being one of the most significant virtual land sales, competing even with the giant Decentraland. From here, it can be seen that this virtual world is no joke; even though the Axie creatures might look cute, there is a massive influx of money in their world. While both Decentraland and The Sandbox have embraced the idea of building, creating, and showing off different created assets, Axie Infinity has rather gone the route of resource farming and breeding for their land, allowing you to also trade and battle the pet Axies in either a PvP or PvE style game (Sandbox, 2021). This makes not only for a rich experience but a rich player base as well, because each of the pets, plots of land, and even such things as love potions can go for a hefty price on the NFT market. This shows how much a niche virtual world can make alongside those of the general audience.

Apart from these three magnates of the virtual gaming world market, there are a few stories of mainstream companies embracing the virtual world idea to create virtual shopping experiences. As we said before, fashion shows are popping up throughout Decentraland, but there's more.

Companies such as Ralph Lauren, Coach, and Tommy Hilfiger have all embraced the idea of virtual shopping experiences to draw in customers. Along with this, Nike has created their own virtual world to expand their consumer base, creating Nikeland to showcase exclusive shoes and other sorts of rare items. Even stores like Dominoes have built small applications within the Decentraland world to order pizza whenever and wherever you are, using Ether or Decentraland's MANA NFT. However, you might embrace these virtual worlds, they are spreading throughout the internet, looking to draw in customers, creators, and socialites alike.

Good Things Come in Small Worlds: Benefits of Virtual Real Estate

Besides the obvious advantage of money-making for its investors and creators, there is always the question of why NFT real estate is advantageous in society? Why is it there? To answer this question, we need to examine what players are doing or playing inside the worlds that they have created or worlds that others have created. What does virtual real estate and the game surrounding it give everyone involved - not just those earning money playing - or are there no benefits to those who do not make money?

The most obvious answer to this question would be socialization. Humans, by nature, are social animals with a craving for interaction and even fun. NFT real estate gives a chance for such a thing to exist without the bounds of centralized governance. This means that within virtual worlds like Decentraland and The Sandbox, the community itself owns and operates the world that it is built-in, giving players the agency to vote, as they see fit, how the world is made up, and decisions about that world.

Apart from this, platforms like Decentraland, The Sandbox, and Axie Infinity all present games and other fun interactive things that make socialization a natural part of the world. This fosters an environment that accepts people into it and makes for a beneficial place to be, as many users of these virtual worlds want for their community and many people in the real world want to escape to.

The next benefit of NFT real estate is the ease with which it can be transferred, overshadowing the outdated system of real estate ownership in the real world (Falcon Rappaport & Berkman, 2021). The benefits of blockchain technology have not been overlooked throughout this book, as it is truly the revolutionary system that the whole industry of crypto tokens has been built upon. This system is also what drives the NFT real estate market.

The advantages of blockchain technology can only be realized once the industries which have emerged from it have succeeded. To move the technology beyond that of NFTs, crypto, and other small blockchain projects, we must invest in NFT real estate, possibly one of the more adventurous projects hosted on the chain.

The last benefit of virtual real estate that we must talk about is the accessibility of the platforms that we see.

Anyone and everyone can be exactly who they want to be within these virtual worlds, allowing for the disabled to interact on the same level as the able-bodied or even those who might be sick at home still be able to interact with friends and family. The Covid-19 Pandemic has made this idea even more approachable as several thousand —maybe even millions — of people were stuck inside their homes in quarantine. These virtual worlds could be the first step to seeing a whole new class of interaction.

CHAPTER 22: CELEBRITIES WHO USE NFTS

C elebrities these days are selling their NFTs for enormous profits. Let's take a look at some of the more well-known names, shall we?

Snoop Dogg

Why aren't we surprised to see him on this list? Since Dogecoin fell, Snoop has been a crypto pumper. On April 2, the rapper announced the release of his NFT collection A Journey with the Dogg. In this sort-of-a-memoir, Snoop chronicles his involvement with the NFT movement from its inception and a new song called "NFT" in addition. New artists in crypto received a share of the profits, while another portion went to his Youth Football League.

Lindsay Lohan

Lindsay is a trendsetter, and you know she's always on top of the newest trends. She was among the first celebrities to embrace NFTs when it was still relatively new in the celebrity world. She also released an NFT, song called "Lullaby" after creating her coins. The EDM track featuring DJ Manual Riva sold for more than $85K in auctions, accompanied by a 'never before seen' animated video clip of the singer with butterflies.

Anthony Pompliano

What's up, crypto momma? Anthony is a Bitcoin lover who specializes in helping out Bitcoin-related startups. He is also one of the newest celebs in NFTs. In February 2019, he released his own CryptoCelebrities NFT. It sold for more than $40K, and each person who bought a share of it received an autographed picture, with all proceeds going to charity.

Kathrine Van Wyk

This NFT is the first Celebrity CryptoArt NFT ever made and sold for $100K in total through auctions on art site Artnome.com. This piece is arguably the most expensive crypto-related item to date. However, there are reports that a similar NFT by a fictional character called "Cryptocelebrities" maybe even more expensive. At any rate, this artwork features a selfie taken by the actress while she was attending Coachella Music Festival 2018 in Indio, California. She's seen wearing bunny ears while flashing the sign of Bunny Gang - one of her favorite cryptocurrency communities.

Lili Simmons

Another celebrity involved in crypto for a while, Lili Simmons, donated a portion of the sales from her NFT to diabetes research. She sold more than $35K worth of this CryptoCelebrities NFT on Artnome, featuring a selfie wearing bunny ears next to Snoop Dogg at Coachella 2018.

Grime

The musician from Canada is raking it in thanks to NFTs. She's already sold more than $6 million worth of WarNymph goods. The collection is now one of the world's most renowned NFTs.

William Shatner

The NFT train was boarded with a selection of photographs drawn from his personal life by Leonard Nimoy's co-star, William Shatner. Given the nonagenarian star's geeky following, his portfolio, which included one photograph of him hugging legendary Leonard Nemoy, sold out completely in 10000 copies.

Paris Hilton

Paris Hilton has embraced NFTswholeheartedly, going all-in in the mode. She's given her dogs names like "Crypto Hilton" and "Ether Reum." The star has sold over a million dollars' worth of NFTs with her latest works Hummingbird in My Metaverse, Iconic Crypto Queen, and Legend of Love.

Ellen DeGeneres

When she sold a cat photo on an NFT market, Crissle demonstrated her interest in the technology. It was promoted on The Ellen Show, and it fetched $33,495, with all proceeds going to World Central Kitchen.

Shawn Mendes

From the sale of his almost signed Fender guitar, neckless vest, keychain, and a slew of other goods, Adel surpassed $600K in NFT. After collaborating with Genies, a prominent avatar brand, Shawn donated money to the Shawn Mendes Foundation Wonder Grants.

Eminem

When Eminem partnered with Nifty Gateway to release his Shady Con NFT in the cryptocurrency industry, he significantly impacted him. Over $1.8 million was paid for the collection of comic books, action figures, and original songs. That isn't all there is to it, though. Sony Music Entertainment and Eminem invested approximately $30 millionin Makers Place, the NFT marketplace.

Mark Cuban

One of the big supporters of cryptocurrency from the beginning is Mark Cuban. So, when the NBA top shots began selling as NFTs, he made over $81K in profits each time one of his sold NFTs was resold.

Jack Dorsey

Jack Dorsey, CEO and Co-Founder of Twitter, sent the first-ever tweet on Twitter. Jack sold the post for a staggering $2.9million. It's all because of NFTs, as insane as it may sound.

Edward Snowden

Finally, let's speak about the torchbearer of today's democracy, who reminded us of the importance of privacy and fought for all of us. Edward Snowden sold his NFT, Stay Free, for 2224 ETH or $7.17 million at publication. The money was given to his Freedom of Press Foundation.

CHAPTER 23:
THE COSTLIEST NFTS

Beeple, Everyday—The First 5000 Days, $69 million

Beeple takes the top spot in this ranking, thanks to the most extraordinary and unexpected sale of this period. Last March 11th, Christie's closed his first online auction in which he has a work NFT that from the initial assessment of $ 100 flies in a very short time to that record of $ 69 million! Beeple Thus finds himself the third living artist most expensive in the world behind himself in Jeff Koons and David Hockney!

Virtual Images of Rick and Morty - $ 2.3 million

Another craftsman who has figured out how to sell showstoppers as NFT at an over-the-top cost is Justin Roiland, the maker of the famous energized arrangement "Rick and Morty." His assortment of 16 masterpieces was sold for 1,300 ETHS, which was near $ 2.3 million.

A part of the closeout returns was dispensed to assisting the needy with peopling in Los Angeles, with Roiland saying it was an approach to test the restrictions of crypto artistry. Strangely, a portion of Roiland's work of art has been delivered in numerous duplicates. Works named "It's Tree Guy" and "Qualified Bachelors" cost $ 10 and $ 100 for each piece, separately. Showstoppers made in a solitary duplicate were sold at greater costs because of their uniqueness and extraordinariness. The play called "The Simpsons" sold for $ 290,100. The closeout's beginning cost was $ 14,999, with its actual being sold for a similar sum.

Land on Axie Infinity - $ 1.5 million

In the first and second positions, we put computerized craftsmanship assortments that were sold through different exchanges. This time, nine land plots on the well-known blockchain game Axie Infinity were sold in a solitary NFT exchange. The client who made the buy paid 888.5 ETH, or $ 1.5 million, at that point. Axie Infinity permits clients to construct a realm in which fabulous characters live. The existence where you can purchase virtual land is called Lunacia and has a set number of spots. The entire plot is separated into 90,601 more modest plots, 19% of which are possessed by players. Hawk called attention to that the land he purchased is in a great area. Moreover, the pattern on Axie Infinity is consistently expanding, as confirmed by the developing number of dynamic clients. Later on, it will likewise be feasible to arrange occasions, like celebrations or shows, on "your territory" and accordingly bring in cash.

Collectible character on CryptoPunks - $ 762,000

Toward the finish of January, an NFT portraying a character from the CryptoPunks game was sold for 605 ETHS, or $ 762,000, at that point. The universe of CryptoPunks is enlivened by crypto artistry development and comprises more than 10,000 extraordinary, advanced characters. Today, they can be purchased and sold in the committed CyberPunks market. It ought to be referenced that already the characters in the game were free, and you simply expected to have an ETH wallet to get them. The NFT - which was initially caught in 2017 and afterward sold at an exorbitant cost - is # 2890. It is a very uncommon 'punk.'

A visit to the blockchain game CryptoKitties - 600 ETH

The following most costly NFT in history is Dragon from the blockchain game CryptoKitties. This adorable, advanced feline was sold for 600 ETHS, or $ 200,000, at that point. Today, a similar measure of tokens costs around 1,000,000 dollars. CryptoKitties is one of the main endeavors to utilize blockchain innovation for diversion. The Axiom Zen studio created it. Like real felines, each virtual feline has a special DNA and its qualities called "credits," which can be given to posterity. Each virtual feline is one of a kind and can't be repeated or moved without the proprietor's permission. As a rule, past ages of virtual felines are viewed as more important. The previously stated makes Dragon uncommon - this is the 10th era of CryptoKitty.

A Delta Time F1 vehicle - $ 110,000

Another NFT is a Formula 1 vehicle on the F1 Delta Time game, explicitly the 1-1-1 model. An unknown gamer purchased this dashing virtual vehicle for an amazing measure of 415.5 ETH. At the hour of procurement, it was more than $ 110,000. Until now, such a measure of ETH is worth around $ 665,000. This buy got the title of the greatest NFT exchange in 2019.

One F1 Delta Time track - $ 200,000

This time, nonetheless, not a vehicle but rather part of a track. Toward the beginning of December 2020, a piece of track on F1 Delta Time was sold for more than 9,000,000 REVV tokens, or $ 200,000, at that point. From that point forward, REVV has developed by 500%, and at the hour of composing this article, it would cost $ 1.2 million for a similar measure of REVV. For F1 Delta Time, all significant game resources are addressed by NFTs. The Circuit de Monaco's virtual track comprises 330 badges of this kind partitioned into four levels - from

"Uncommon" to "Summit." Each token addresses a virtual track share, giving its proprietor a bunch of advantages. For this specific NFT, it was at the "Zenith" level. Its purchaser will get 5% of all in-game income and 4.2% of first-class marking benefits from player stores. Both will be paid in REVV utility tokens.

NFT guarantee Money Insurance - 350 ETH

"5000.0 ETH-Cover-NFT" is a protection strategy dependent on yinsure. Money, an undertaking upheld by Yearn.Finance. Because of an enthusiastic advanced approach, its proprietor profits by protection against mistakes in keen agreements on Curve.fi up to 5,000 ETH. NFT costs 350 ETHS, which compares to more than $ 560,000 today. Yinsure is otherwise called Cover. So, it is a consolidated protection inclusion ensured by Nexus Mutual and another sort of tokenized protection. Protection approaches are represented as NFT. Every one of them is a special NFT, otherwise called NFT, and can be moved, purchased, or sold.

12,600 square meters of virtual land in Decentraland - 514 ETH

Somebody purchased 12,600 m2 for 514 ETHS on the Decentraland blockchain game. The game is an Ethereum-based decentralized augmented experience stage. Its clients can make, analyze, and adapt their substance and applications. Decentraland has a restricted 3D virtual space called LAND. It is a non-fungible computerized resource kept up by Ethereum shrewd agreements. The landowner has full control of their virtual land.

Land at 22.2 in Decentraland - 345 ETH

Here is Decentraland once more. This time it's a land parcel in a "great area" at 22.2. In the realm of Decentraland, the size of the land is fixed. About 80% of its space is private, and the vast majority of the rest is sold and rented by Decentraland. The excess land, like streets and squares, doesn't have a place with anybody. Players can just walk their characters on their territory and public land, so the situation is very significant. Parts found nearer to well-known regions will be more costly than those situated in more distant zones. Taking a gander at how quickly the NFT markets are developing and what costs non-fungible tokens are sold, we can accept that this will be another gigantic pattern just after Defi. A significant quality of NFTs is that each has its own remarkable and interesting attributes. NFTs are yet a specialty showcase, however have effectively discovered numerous applications.

CHAPTER 24:
NFT MYTHS DEBUNKED AND OTHER POTENTIAL CONS REVEALED

Myths, legends, and all kinds of stories have permeated through the NFT community and have become one of the few things that mainstream media has associated with NFTs in general. This, like many media myths and legends, need to be disproved. To do this, we will be exploring some of the more common ones that affect the community at large and looking at why they might see it this way, then we'll disprove them with a look at our perspective. Additionally, we will explore some of the cons that might be affecting the NFT community and market while also exploring ways we might reduce their effects.

The first mention of NFTs in mainstream media has been quiet recently, with the first real presence of the term coming into notice in the last couple of years. Before NFTs, there were cryptocurrencies, which also experienced a bad rap for the last few years in mainstream media, so in turn, there was quite a bit of lumping together, which happened to put NFTs in a bad light.

Now, though NFTs are gaining a lot of traction every day, there still might be a lot of less-than-great opinions on the matter. This can all be overturned by debunking myths in this chapter and the support that NFTs need in other chapters.

Debunked and Disproved: Popular Myths of NFTs

Misconceptions abound when speaking on the topic of NFTs. There have been many claims to many different things related to NFTs, but most of the mainstream ones are either totally misconstrued or not entirely true. But how do you go about separating the real myths from the fake myths when so many exist in the first place?

The first myth that is always spouted when brought up in mainstream media is the idea that "NFTs are not valuable." Hopefully, with the examples of Beeple, Decentraland, or CryptoKitties, you can find this to be at least false in practice.

In theory, NFTs are valuable for two simple reasons: the existence of the smart contract and the concept of scarcity. As with anything related to the blockchain, it is secure and safe. The security that we find in the blockchain is then transferred directly to the value of the things it hosts, acting as a funhouse mirror to the risk of an asset on the stock market.

For example, an NFT made off-chain and hosted by some third party can be thought of as a risky investment; however, if that asset were hosted entirely on-chain, the investment would be less risky. The funhouse part comes with the fact that risk is usually tied to return, but with NFTs, it is the opposite. The more secure an asset, the more it's worth. The same idea applies to the concept of scarcity. Scarcity acts as a value enhancer even more than security does, being the primary tool with which investors drive the value of their assets. This is because security can easily create scarcity.

For example, say there is an asset being sold on a trusted market, then that asset gets copied to another, less-trusted market by a morally compromised investor. In a world without the security of the blockchain, that asset would then simply be worth nothing because of the ease of copying it and distributing it elsewhere. However, this is not the case, and the blockchain's security does exist to drive the scarcity of an asset.

So, in the case of the replicated piece, there would be a parsing process by the nodes of the blockchain that would pick up the transaction history of the asset and assure the scarcity of that piece to only one. Then, because the asset is the only one in existence and it's hosted on-chain, the value of that piece is assured of going up, giving NFTs their value as assets.

The second common myth that is spread around is the idea that NFTs are too complicated for the beginner oreven the intermediate investor. Many media sources will tell you that there is no reason to join in the money that NFT offers due to the complexity that it suffers, and the learning curve is too steep for any casual investor. This is simply not true.

With the introduction of many new marketplaces every day, there have been constant updates to the user experience and overall ease of access to the NFT trade. Buying and selling NFTs has been made all the easier with auctions running every day, a friendly interface to greet you, and new crypto wallets that allow for an easy first-day setting up.

This is then just the beginning as many markets and platforms are transferring themselves to mainstream devices like browser extensions and even mobile phones, giving NFTs a step up in the mountain climb to provide consumers access to their products. Furthermore, the practice of minting an NFT has also become one of the simpler processes in the whole of the NFT trade. This is because creators drive the market and create the product that both investors and markets wish to sell; without the ease to do this, there would be no trade in the first place.

For example, Open Sea's lazy minting process is arguably one of the easiest ways to mint an NFT, so much so that any artist with work in digital work would know how to do it. This creates a very healthy atmosphere for anyone looking to become a creator of NFTs, removing almost all the steepness of the learning curve.

The third myth that has seen a recent resurgence of popularity in the last few years has been the idea that NFTs are bad for the environment. This is a myth that is not entirely true, and the magnitude at which people accuse NFTs is simply an overreaction. People believe that NFTs consume an immense amount of power per transaction and the idea that NFTs need to have a particular node on the blockchain contributes to this myth.

The simple fact of the matter is that the whole of the blockchain requires this power. There is no change in power consumption if the transactions of NFTs are increased; instead, the blockchain's power consumption stays the same. As we have said before, this technology has the capacity to change the world into a better place; however, this facet of it is giving the concept a bad rap. There is constant work to reduce the consumption of the blockchain which is essentially the real problem at hand. There is no need for the media to put off the idea of NFTs in reaction to a problem that affects us all.

The last myth we'll explore is the crux of arguments against NFTs, giving them a hard measure of worthless hate and misunderstanding. This myth is the idea that NFTs as art forms are pointless. We have already proved that NFTs are valuable with the idea of security and scarcity; however, there is also the concept that NFTs are not useful at all, and even art made in their form is pointless.

To counter this, we need just look at some of the NFTs submitted in the last few years, works of art that are essentially just one and one with digital art but under the tokenized moniker. This means that as art, NFTs are the exact same as other pieces of work, maybe even going so far as to replace modern standards for how art is sold.

This is what we must think about when the myth of pointlessness is attributed to the NFT trade, as the more artists and buyers come rushing in to create, buy, and collect, the more the myth has no weight in the matter. As for the future of NFTs at this point in time, we can see a huge rise coming on, moving both art and technology forward. These myths and legends of NFTs are some of the few things holding back the advancement of the industry and are ultimately bad for the blockchain economy as a whole. If we look to better NFTs, we will be bettering crypto and blockchain just the same. Avoid the myths and lies told by those who wish to drag the industry down and instead focus on the existing problems of blockchain and NFTs, working to better them and the community.

The Real Cons of NFTs

You might think it silly to embrace the problems within the NFT industry in a book about NFTs, and you might rather look to avoid them, however, this should not be the attitude we have. It is always important to realize where you fall short and where you should look to make it better. This means that we will be exploring some of the common problems with NFTs that many of us in the community have realized and want to fix. This list of problems is by no means exhaustive, but I would purport that each of these items has the most actively workable solutions that could be implemented by a combined effort from many in the community. The first problem that we will talk about is the amount of power it takes to host the blockchain

Though it is a crypto-wide problem, it affects NFTs, particularly because of the myths surrounding their association. Because we have this situation, we as a community must help with this glaring problem, mostly by supporting the blockchain itself. This might sound counterintuitive; however, it is needed to make the blockchain a less power-consuming entity as the research done by people working with the blockchain need the money support to fix it.

Without the buying and selling of NFTs, there is no capital to fund research into a way to make the blockchain more efficient. So, even though the hosting of NFTs might contribute to the problem in a minor way, there is the need to fund the blockchain technology itself to help pay to fix it.

The second problem of NFTs is how reliant the market is on trends and momentary popularity.

Many investors have said this many times before, and some of it is false, but the role trends have in the market is bigger than some might think. Because much of the market is based on subjective demographics and traits, there is little room for the extrinsic value that drives the sales of the NFTs. This means that if a trend emerges in the whole community, the trend turns into a driving force of the market for a short period of time, all because the traits of the trend are what people want. This also means that many investors will see the market as too risky to invest in or too speculative.

If we are going to fix this problem, we must see the value of art, gather up worthwhile artists, and expand the horizons of NFTs. Seeing the value of art itself isn't the easiest answer to this problem, but if we understand that art has benefits to people's lives, we might create a less risky market. Additionally, if we keep vetting artists with better metrics, allowing only those who wish to make the NFT trade better, we can increase the amount of good NFTs to buy. Finally, if we expand the reach of products beyond just digital art and beyond the blockchain community, we can muster up the people who might keep the trade going.

A third problem of the NFT trade is the presence of less-than-reliable platforms that allow copying of content to their sites. This is an inherent problem with NFTs that isn't without its fixes. Some might say that the blockchain shouldn't allow this problem because the transaction history should prevent it, but that is not always the case. The key to preventing copying a token to other sites is for the next site to take into account what is being minted; without fail-safes in place to find copied work, the reputation of NFTs goes down. For example, say an amateur artist creates a very well-done piece with it being near exclusive to that site, but another site has very lax rules on copied material.

There is then a scammer who takes the piece that the artist made by copying it through simple copying means and then posts it for sale in the lax marketplace, allowing for it to be sold at a much lower rate than it is worth. This not only reduces the total amount that that artist will receive on their work in the exclusive market due to a lack of scarcity, but this also floods the market with low-class copies, supporting the lax marketplace. The fix, in turn, is to instill an ethics system in the NFT market while at the same time putting rules and codes in place to prevent the problem from happening. Policing the lax markets and increasing the overall good that NFTs are doing.

The fourth and final problem with NFTs is the lack of control given to their owners and creators. Just because you have purchased a digital art NFT, there is no guarantee that you will be able to manipulate copies or even the original artwork. This means that the idea of ownership can be misconstrued from other forms of ownership and the buyers and sellers might be turned away from the concept of NFTs.

If you do not already know about this, it is important that you know that the NFT is what you own and not the artwork itself. This means that any rights that a creator might have been not yours to take. You cannot change theartwork to suit your needs and keep selling it as an NFT, nor can you make copies of it without the express permission of the actual owners; this all represents a problem for the NFT trade in that there isn't much stock to be managed.

A way to fix this would be to give a sort of decision-making tool to the buyers and owners, one with which owners can decide what to do with the NFT they own or at least have a say in it. This way, the original creators retain control while keeping investors happy.

The fact that the community has a long way to go means that there is potential waiting to be tapped into in the many different facets of the NFT markets. The myths are one step back and several steps forward, still only being driven by the unaware media. The problems that we do realize are glaring but not insurmountable. These two in and of themselves give meaning to us as investors, as without them, there would not be a trend of popularity growing inside both the media and the community at large.

This trend is what makes for committed members of the community who want to stay in it for the long haul, so even though the market is a speculative one, there is still a chance for people to stay. Even though the effects of the blockchain's energy consumption can weigh on everyone, there are still answers to be found in the funding of the technology's potential. Though there are marketplaces out there that might look to take advantage of collectors, investors, and creators alike, there are many different growing marketplaces that give their users a plethora of benefits. Despite the fact that problems and myths are surrounding the NFT trade, there are solutions and truths that exist as well.

CONCLUSION

NFT marketplaces are becoming increasingly popular, and it doesn't appear to be slowing down anytime soon. With more unique projects that allow collectors to invest in unique pieces or games, next-generation digital art collections are drawing a larger number of investors than ever before. If you're interested in selling your artwork online, we've provided some simple guidelines for getting started.

If you're looking to invest in the expanding cryptocurrency market, hundreds of unique options are available through dozens of exchanges.

With the advent of NFTs in several sectors, it's critical to grasp how they operate and what prospects exist. Non-Fungible Tokens have been praised as a potential solution to digitally preserving art collections while maintaining their inherent characteristics.

They can also establish a whole gaming world that allows players to enjoy video

games in new ways. In the same vein, NFTs have been employed in several other sectors that may not be as readily apparent. In short, they can establish a whole new world.

NFTs are also an opportunity for the future of art and investment, but there's more to it than that. They represent a complex framework for future digital collectibles. The marketplace for these digital assets is constantly expanding, which means it's critical to be aware of the various new opportunities as they emerge.

Made in United States
Orlando, FL
09 May 2022

17681448R00076